NEW YORK

AUTHENTIC RECIPES CELEBRATING THE FOODS OF THE WORLD

Recipes and Text
CAROLYNN CARREÑO

Photographs
QUENTIN BACON

General Editor
CHUCK WILLIAMS

Bonnier Books

CONTENTS

RECIPES

INTRODUCTION

From the first hot dog sold on the street to this season's duck carved at table at the Four Seasons, New York cuisine has always reflected the enterprising spirit on which the city was founded. The food scene continues to embody this culinary creativity, along with an attitude that embraces every global influence.

CULINARY HISTORY

New York City's status as a global centre of finance, art, architecture, theatre, media, and cuisine is so well established that one rarely stops to think of how it came to be so. At its founding, New York was a place in which free-thinking was encouraged and often rewarded economically. Thus, since the first Dutch settlers, the city has been shaped by risk-taking entrepreneurs and a populace willing to consider the merits of anything new and untested. This sensibility fostered a culture, and by extension a cuisine, that was an amalgam of Old World tradition and New World innovation and, over time, was shaped by a continuous flow of immigrants from around the globe.

The city's extraordinary rise to prominence is put into perspective when you consider that the Dutch purchased Manhattan, an island thickly forested to the water's edge, from the Native Americans less than four hundred years ago. The area's rich natural resources – forests teeming with deer, boar and turkeys; rivers brimming with salmon, shad and bass – attracted hard-working farmers and merchants from Europe. Because of the city's

location at the mouth of the Hudson River, New Amsterdam, as the early settlement was called, quickly became a hub. By the mid-1600s, two markets were in operation, and by the end of the 1700s, a successful system of public markets was in place. The harbour facilitated the import and export of goods, making the city a worldwide centre for trade. Briefly, after the American Revolution, New York even served as the nation's capital.

As a settlement populated by immigrants, New York did not have an indigenous cuisine. Enterprising innkeepers opened taverns modelled after those in England, and Germans ran beer halls and wine gardens. Food was served from a set menu that included boiled meat and vegetables and oysters on the half-shell, fried or in a stew. The shellfish were so abundant in New York Harbour that oyster-gathering was the main occupation on Staten Island until 1810, when the beds were exhausted.

Much of the culinary landscape that is associated with New York began to develop with the waves of immigrants who arrived in

the mid-1800s. Many were escaping religious persecution or poverty; sometimes entire villages emigrated together, creating their own enclaves in the city. The Chinese, who started to arrive in the 1850s, offered their regional fare in small, inexpensive restaurants. The Irish, fleeing the potato famine around the same time, contributed porterhouses, where customers could imbibe house-brewed beer. These immigrants originated many foods that continue to be identified with New York. Jews invented pastrami and corned beef as a way of preserving meat. Italian grocers made pizzas as an alternative and profitable use for their bread dough and coal-fired brick ovens.

Meanwhile, another side of New York society was taking shape. The late 1800s were boom years, when the steel, oil and shipping industries produced America's first millionaires. This was the beginning of upper-class culture, an era known for its conspicuous consumption. At the culinary centre was Delmonico's. Opened by two Swiss brothers in 1827, Delmonico's was the country's first dedicated restaurant (one not

attached to an inn), where diners could order à la carte. The restaurant introduced New Yorkers to the finest in French cooking, including roast canvasback duck (a local delicacy at the time) partridges stuffed with truffles and vegetables simmered in cream. Thus began the city's fascination with French culture and cuisine.

New York's high society was known to sit down to as many as five meals a day, inspiring such alternatives to Delmonico's as the Waldorf-Astoria, Café Martin, Sherry's and Astor House. Many were staffed by former Delmonico's employees but, until Prohibition forced its closure in 1923, Delmonico's was the standard-bearer. A special dinner was held at the restaurant for Charles Dickens, who on an earlier visit to the city had complained of American food. After the feast, which featured over forty dishes, the writer retracted his statement. Samuel F. B. Morse sent the first telegrams to Europe from Delmonico's and Diamond Jim Brady was reputed to be a regular.

New York's love of French cuisine was revived after the 1939 World's Fair. The popularity of the Fair's French pavilion inspired the restaurant that was perhaps the most influential in the city's history: Le Pavillion. Its impact on the restaurant scene reverberated through the voice of Pierre Franey, who came to New York to cook at Le Pavillion and became legendary as the *New York Times'* 60 Minute Gourmet. Throughout the 1960s, thanks to Le Pavillion and its numerous offshoots – La Côte Basque, La Grenouille, and La Caravelle – haute cuisine came to mean French cuisine.

At the same time, New York was being introduced to international flavours through the cookery books of James Beard and the *New York Times* critic Craig Claiborne. Both helped to demystify haute cuisine and legitimate the influence of other world cuisines.

In 1959, when restaurateur Joseph Baum opened the legendary Four Seasons in Midtown, he pioneered the concept of a new American cuisine – a cuisine that reflected New York as the crossroads of all cultures.

The Four Seasons menu folded the ingredients and preparations from a variety of cuisines into classic American and French dishes. It was an epic departure at the time, a precursor to the fusion cuisine of recent decades and to the direction that New York's food scene has continued to follow.

Although New York gained its reputation as the food capital of the United States at the turn of the twentieth century, the city's palate has become truly global in the years since World War II. In the 1940s and 1950s, Puerto Ricans and Dominicans settled in East Harlem, and African-Americans from the South landed in Harlem, bringing their distinctive culinary traditions with them. Since the 1970s, immigrants from Bangladesh, Korea, Thailand, the Philippines, Latin America, Pakistan, Haiti, and Jamaica have created their own neighbourhoods, and their influence has trickled into the mainstream, making once-exotic dishes such as pad Thai, kimchee, and empanadas integral to New Yorkers' culinary vocabulary.

CONTEMPORARY CUISINE

New York cuisine evolves as quickly as every other aspect of the city, yet it is rooted in centuries of tradition. It is not surprising that the rest of the country looks to the New York food scene for a glimpse of the future of the nation's table.

As a place largely defined by change and by the creative people drawn here to make their mark, New York has seen a number of fleeting culinary trends. During the 1980s, a decade known for its brash excess, cutting-edge restaurants such as The Quilted Giraffe married French techniques with avant-garde Japanese-inspired presentations. At Gotham Bar and Grill, where chef Alfred Portale started the "vertical food movement", main dishes were stacked and layered ever higher in ring moulds and architectural desserts were crowned with arches of spun sugar.

One culinary movement from the 1980s still defines New York cuisine today. It is comfort food, which can be traced to the Union Square Café. Ample portions of well-prepared, home-style dishes such as meat loaf, roast chicken, and mashed potatoes may have been a reaction to the popularity of nouvelle cuisine or perhaps a response to the stock market crash of 1987. Regardless of what brought it on, comfort food stuck. Today, mashed potatoes are ubiquitous at even the finest restaurants, and a well-prepared roast chicken may garner even more respect than any elaborate French presentation.

Comfort food owes its origins to the revolution touting simple preparations of local, seasonal ingredients that started in California in the 1970s. Jonathan Waxman, who had worked at Chez Panisse with Alice Waters in the late 1970s, introduced this so-called food revolution to New York in the 1980s at Jams. The movement has had a profound effect.

The best of the city's chefs shop at regional farmers' markets and build their menus around specialities brought in from Long Island, New Jersey and the Hudson River Valley. New Yorkers are always on the hunt for artisans and the food they produce. Word of a talented new baker or chocolatier in the city, or a cheese-producer or wine-maker on Long Island, spreads quickly.

Although the region's harsh climate could be seen as a setback for cooking with local ingredients, New Yorkers love the changing seasons and gladly honour them with a decided shift in what they cook and eat. Residents gear up for each season's culinary offerings: spring's tender asparagus, rampions, and rhubarb; followed by summer's first vine-ripened tomatoes, juicy peaches, and sweet-corn; then autumn's Concord grapes, Seckel pears, and quince. Winter's short days and cold weather promise their own romance, calling for hearty bean soups, slow-cooked meat, caramelised roasted root vegetables, and simple desserts such as bread pudding.

The progression of the seasons fosters a particular affinity for fruit. New arrivals on the market are eagerly anticipated and are ripe with culinary possibilities. Crumbles, cobblers, pies, and compotes might remain reliable fixtures on restaurant menus, but the fruits with which they are made will change from berries to cherries, then to peaches and plums, and finally to pears and apples as the calendar moves on. At the Four Seasons, the fruit sauce served alongside the signature Long

Island duck changes, along with the foliage in the restaurant, four times a year.

Despite the presence of a pulsating drive towards what is new and hip, classic dishes are afforded the utmost respect. Even the most highly regarded chefs would be viewed askance without a few homespun New York classics to anchor their menus. These items are elevated by the quality of the ingredients and the care with which they are made: matzo ball soup might be prepared with organic, free-range chicken; macaroni and cheese (a favourite from the beloved Horn & Hardart Automats that once peppered the city's business districts) would be updated with artisanally produced Vermont cheese topped with fresh truffle shavings; cheesecake would be sweetened with pure maple syrup from upstate New York.

Chefs and diners have always relied on European culinary traditions to shape their definition of haute cuisine. Even though quite a few of New York's reigning French restaurants, namely, Lutèce, La Côte Basque, and

La Caravelle have closed their doors, the reverence for French cuisine can still be seen at every level. All of New York's four-star restaurants are French, and replicas of casual French bistros and the fare they typically serve – *steak au poivre* and *frites,* frisée salad with *lardons,* and profiteroles with bittersweet chocolate sauce – can be found in almost every Manhattan neighbourhood.

More recently, Italian cuisine has become the culinary wellspring of choice. In addition to the Italian-American restaurants in Italian neighbourhoods in all five boroughs, restaurants serving authentic, regional Italian fare are found throughout the city. Places such as Babbo Ristorante e Enoteca in Greenwich Village and Beppe near Union Square take the principles of simply prepared Italian food to heights of richness and complexity that would be foreign in the Old Country but which capture the attention of New Yorkers' adventurous and sophisticated palates.

The no-nonsense attitude for which New Yorkers are known has kept fusion cuisine

from taking hold, unlike in other parts of the country. Many such restaurants have opened in New York, but they almost systematically meet with failure. Judging by those that have endured, New Yorkers are not averse to the comingling of culinary influences. Yet they demand some stability. Their preference is for a cuisine that is rooted in one tradition and shows only the subtlest influences of others, as is the case at the Japanese-based Nobu in Tribeca and Daniel Boulud's French-focused DB Bistro Moderne in Midtown.

New Yorkers have earned a reputation for rarely cooking at home, but when they prepare food in their own kitchens, they do so with gusto. Friday night, when restaurants are packed largely with a non-local crowd, is a favourite evening for eating at home. When New Yorkers entertain, the menu is well thought out and frequently challenging. It would not be uncommon to take an entire day to prepare the meal. Cooks may even replicate a dish, such as miso-marinated cod, that they enjoyed in a local restaurant.

EATING OUT

Eating at a restaurant is a form of entertainment. Whether New Yorkers are dining at a casual neighbourhood trattoria, a classic steakhouse or a much-lauded restaurant opened by a celebrity chef, restaurants are the stage on which they play out their social lives.

The late Joseph Baum, creator of the famed Four Seasons restaurant, is quoted as saying, "People don't come to our restaurants because they're hungry". Diners flocked to Baum's Four Seasons and his many other theme-oriented restaurants because entering the highly designed spaces was like walking on to a stage set. To eat amid such surroundings was to participate in an ongoing, unscripted theatre performance featuring innovative, well-executed cuisine. The same formula dominates many of New York's finest restaurants today.

For many New Yorkers, eating out is not reserved only for special occasions. Typically, living space is small, making cooking and entertaining somewhat difficult, so New Yorkers use restaurants as their kitchens and dining rooms away from home. They catch up with friends and celebrate birthdays and business deals in restaurants, eat solo at restaurant bars, order take-away from restaurants and even host dinner parties in the restaurants' private rooms and chef's tables.

Restaurants line all but the quietest residential streets and, in their abundant variety, appeal to every ethnic craving from Thai to Tibetan food and to every price range. New Yorkers like to say that eating at inexpensive eateries, such as a local falafel joint or a Chinese restaurant, costs less than cooking at home. For New Yorkers who brag about how long it has been since they last turned on their ovens or stocked their refrigerators, it is not uncommon to eat out three meals a day.

The unorthodox working hours of many New Yorkers are reflected in the number of people enjoying a leisurely cup of coffee on a weekday morning in neighbourhood diners and cafés. For those with office jobs, breakfast is generally a grab-and-go cup of coffee and a buttered roll from a street vendor, or a latte and pastry from a convenient bakery on the way to work. Lunchtime is similarly routine. In Midtown and Soho, employees of investment banks, fashion houses, publishers, law firms, and television networks pour out of their offices and crowd the classier soup, salad, and sandwich shops. Executives lunch at swankier spots such as the 44 at the Royalton Hotel or Lever House in Midtown.

Dinner, however, is the meal New Yorkers stop to enjoy as the reward for the daily grind. On a casual weeknight, they choose from among the myriad restaurants within a few blocks of their homes, frequenting those where they know in advance what they will order and where they receive special treatment. This might be a favourite sushi bar, a friendly Thai café, or a trattoria where the year's first dinner enjoyed at an outdoor table marks the coming of spring.

For city residents, Thursday nights are considered the best on which to dine out because visitors from New Jersey, Long Island, Westchester County or the outer boroughs – known as the "bridge-and-tunnel crowd" – descend upon Manhattan on Friday and Saturday evenings. Thursday is the night New Yorkers often reserve for trying a new

restaurant they have just read about in *New York Magazine* or the *New York Times*.

For large groups, eating at chef's tables and kitchen tables promises a view of the action. This style of dining out is standard in better restaurants in France and Italy, but only about ten years ago did Maguy Le Coze, the owner of Le Bernadin, introduce this form of kitchen theatre to New York. At Le Cirque 2000, a semi-circular banquette is situated unobtrusively in a corner of the kitchen, which is as opulent as the main dining room. At Barbuto in the West Village, Jonathan Waxman serves guests himself, family-style, at a long rustic table in the kitchen.

Despite the frequency with which they eat out, New Yorkers typically reserve certain restaurants for special occasions. Steakhouses such as The Palm on the East Side and Peter Luger in Brooklyn, which epitomise old New York, are ideal places to take friends, family or business associates, especially those from out-of-town. Entertaining visitors presents the perfect excuse to revisit landmarks such as

Katz's Delicatessen, Sylvia's Soul Food, and Chumley's, the Greenwich Village speakeasy. Dinner at four-star restaurants, which are exclusively French and are characterised by white tablecloths and formal service, often lasts two or three hours. Thus, a visit to Daniel, Aureole, or Jean Georges is a rare treat, to be savoured infrequently by even the most food-obsessed New Yorkers.

New Yorkers' taste in dining is becoming progressively more casual. Whereas opulent rooms and stuffy service were once the benchmarks of fine dining, many of today's favourite restaurants, including Babbo Ristorante e Enoteca, Craft, and Gramercy Tavern, widely considered among the best in the city, are decidedly more relaxed – and more reflective of contemporary tastes.

Diners with a preference for the casual can select from a seemingly boundless choice of ethnic restaurants, especially if they travel to the boroughs outside Manhattan. Nearly every cuisine around the world, from Korean and Cambodian to Cuban and Peruvian to

East Indian and West African, can be found in this city of immigrants. These authentic, often family-run establishments provide a glimpse into the traditions of other cultures. The atmosphere is casual, to say the least, but the prices are inexpensive, even if the decor leaves something to be desired.

In recent years, however, ethnic food has become well established in mainstream restaurants. Many, like Nam, a stylish Vietnamese restaurant in Tribeca, and Bond Street, a hip East Village sushi bar, appeal to New Yorkers who are quite willing to pay a little extra to trade in the linoleum-tiled floors and fluorescent lighting of some of the more modest ethnic eateries for romantic, atmospheric surroundings where the interior design is emphasised as much as the quality of the food. Many of the new restaurants – including Kittichai, a new Thai restaurant in Soho, Spice Market in the Meat-packing District, which serves updated south-east Asian cuisine and Matsuri in Chelsea, specialising in Japanese cuisine – almost qualify as theme restaurants.

MARKETS

New York's food aficionados willingly travel to purchase exactly what they desire. They visit farmers' markets for the best local produce and seafood, seek out small producers in the city's historic neighbourhoods and frequent the many speciality shops selling foods imported from all over the world.

Every day of the week, all year long, New Yorkers can shop for locally-grown food at farmers' markets in all five boroughs of the city. At stalls set up in parks, squares, playgrounds and parking lots, vendors display foods from farms in the Hudson River Valley, Long Island and New Jersey or harvested from local waters. The bounty is quite impressive: myriad vegetables and fruits in their seasonal prime; lobsters, scallops, skate and bluefish fished off Long Island; fresh and aged artisanal cheeses; free-range chickens, ducks and eggs; maple syrup, just-baked pastries, pies, breads and homemade jams and preserves.

Before these farmers' markets were established in the 1970s, local farmers had no easy outlet to consumers in the city, and New Yorkers had no access to local seasonal produce. Barry Benepe, a New York architect and planner, saw that the number of family farms in the region was diminishing due to the pressures of agribusiness and land development. Benepe and his colleague Bob Lewis approached the Council on the Environment of New York City with the idea of starting a farmers' market in New York to bridge the gap between area farmers and the city's large consumer base. The first Greenmarket, as they are now called, opened in 1976 on a city-owned plot at Fifty-ninth Street and Second Avenue with a handful of farmers. Today, the council sponsors markets in more

than thirty locations, most of them open year-round, others only during the spring and summer growing season.

The Union Square Greenmarket, at Broadway and East Seventeenth Street, is by far the largest, hosting some seventy farmers at the peak of the season. Open four days a week – Monday, Wednesday, Friday, and Saturday – it is the epicentre of New York's food scene. Restaurateur Danny Meyer even chose this location for his first restaurant, Union Square Café, due to the proximity to the Greenmarket and its quality fruits and vegetables. In the early morning hours, while many farmers are still setting up their stands, restaurant chefs in their chef's whites can be seen intently examining the seasonal specialities, choosing ingredients for market-based specials and market menus (page 97). For food-loving New Yorkers, a trip to the market has become a necessary ritual; they come with empty shopping bags and baskets and leave loaded down with unusual varieties of vegetables and fruits they would never find in their neighbourhood greengrocer's.

The growing appreciation for foods made by small producers has spawned other markets. Chelsea Market, opened in 1997, is a long indoor concourse that runs between Ninth and Tenth Avenues on Seventeenth Street. It contains more than twenty small shops including Lobster Place, offering fresh seafood, and Buon Italia, selling a broad

range of imported Italian foods. The market serves as a direct-from-the-source outlet for ice cream, yoghurt and dairy produce from Ronnybrook Farm Dairy. Baked goods from Amy's Breads, Eleni's Cookies and Fat Witch Brownies are all made on the premises, many in open kitchens that provide a culinary performance for the shopper to admire. Appropriately, the building was once the factory in which the National Biscuit Company produced the first Oreo cookies, a biscuit that became an American institution.

Another recent arrival is the Grand Central Market, which opened in 1999 in the beautifully restored Grand Central Station in Midtown. Before their trains depart, commuters can pick up cheese from Murray's Cheese Shop, confectionery from Li-Lac Chocolates, meat from Koglin, a German butcher, and other foods from a dozen, mostly independently-owned, vendors.

New York is also home to many of the nation's leading gourmet food stores, including Zabar's, an Upper West Side institution on

Broadway and Eightieth Street since the 1930s and the object of New Yorkers' enduring affection. Zabar's, known for quality smoked fish, imported foods, a cheese department that was ahead of its time, and house-roasted coffee, developed a loyal following among the affluent Jewish population of the Upper West Side. In the 1970s, Zabar's began selling appliances and kitchen gadgets, for which it is now equally famous. The store is run by Saul and Stanley Zabar, two of the three sons of the original owner. The youngest son, Eli Zabar, is owner of the Vinegar Factory (among other ventures), a classy gourmet food emporium on the other side of Central Park.

Another pioneering speciality food shop is Dean & DeLuca, which Joel Dean and Giorgio DeLuca opened in 1977 in SoHo, which was then a relatively deserted artists' neighbourhood. The two founders were committed to offering the best foodstuffs in the world to the city's increasingly discerning population. They travelled the globe looking for unusual and

high-quality products to stock their shop and claimed to be the first to sell balsamic vinegar and sun-dried tomatoes, among other now common items, in the United States. Today, visiting Dean & DeLuca is like going to a culinary museum, and a trip to the expanded location on Prince Street and Broadway is a must for visitors interested in food.

New York is a city of speciality shopping, and residents regularly take advantage of the many ethnic enclaves and shops. For a Russian food experience, they travel to Brighton Beach, called Little Odessa, to visit M & I International or any of the other outlets on Brighton Beach Avenue known for Russian specialities such as black bread, smoked fish, sausages, pickles, stuffed fried breads, and borscht. A holiday or special occasion might inspire a trip to Manhattan's Lower East Side to Guss' Pickles or Russ & Daughters for smoked fish. A particular meal requiring unusual ingredients provides the perfect excuse to go to Atlantic Avenue in Brooklyn for Middle Eastern ingredients, to the West

African Grocery on Manhattan's Ninth Avenue, to the Curry Hill section of Lexington Avenue for Indian spices or to the many Chinatown supermarkets that sell foods from a number of Asian cultures.

A visit to the Arthur Avenue Retail Market, a covered market that sprawls over seven square blocks in the Belmont neighbourhood of the Bronx, is popular not only because of the vast selection of home-made and imported foods sold there and on the surrounding streets, but also because the experience is a trip back in time to an old-fashioned Italian-American community. Known as Little Italy in the Bronx, the market was opened by Mayor Fiorello La Guardia in 1940 to provide indoor stalls for Italian vendors selling from barrows on the streets. Many of the family-owned stalls in the bustling marketplace, such as Teitel Brothers, a grocery store, and Madonia Brothers Bakery, date back almost a hundred years. Calabria Pork Store, Casa Della Mozzarella, Mike's Deli and Borgatti's Ravioli and Egg Noodles are known for quality and the kind of friendly service found only where the owner is on the premises and the clientele are regulars. The market is open every day except Sunday, but is at its best on Saturday mornings, when many of the shop-owners and regular customers who have since moved out to the suburbs come back to visit the old neighbourhood.

FLAVOURS OF NEW YORK CITY

New Yorkers often think of their city as a series of small villages, each having a unique history and flavour. Going to Manhattan's Lower East Side for a pastrami sandwich or to Brooklyn for a bowl of Vietnamese noodles is to get a taste of the real New York.

Tribeca and the Financial District

Early in the city's history, Tribeca (Triangle below Canal Street) was called Washington Market. The market itself remained active for two centuries, until the 1950s, and vestiges of the area's former days as a centre for wholesale produce are still visible today. The renovated lofts in Tribeca are now some of the most coveted residential space in the city. For some years, the neighbourhood has been home to a number of New York's finest restaurants. The pioneer was undoubtedly a fancy French restaurant called Chanterelle, which opened in 1979 and remains in the same location, not far from Ground Zero, the former site of the World Trade Center. At the more casual end of the dining spectrum is Bubby's, a retro, Americana-style restaurant that has expanded over the years to become a neighbourhood institution. The area continues to draw diners to such high-profile restaurants as Bouley, 66, Montrachet, The Harrison, Danube, and Nobu.

Further south, the Financial District in Lower Manhattan remains the city's historical centre, evidenced by landmarks such as the historic Fraunces Tavern, where George Washington bid farewell to his officers in 1783, still serving drinks. The New York Stock Exchange, founded in 1817, moved to its

current building in 1903. Some large financial institutions have moved to Midtown, but artists and young entrepreneurs have replaced them and breathed new life into the restaurant scene. Bazzini, which has been roasting nuts for the wholesale trade for more than a hundred years, has opened a grocery and café catering to the neighbourhood's new residents. In 1999, Delmonico's, the country's first dedicated restaurant, reopened its doors near its original Williams Street location.

Chinatown

Governed by its own rhythms, Chinatown, an ever-expanding area on the eastern side of Lower Manhattan, seems a world away from the city, yet very much a part of it. Over the years, other Asian immigrants, mostly Thai and Vietnamese, have settled in the neighbourhood and opened restaurants and groceries. Pressed ducks hang in shop windows, and street vendors sell many types of noodles and dumplings. Some restaurants do not have menus in English, and the dishes delivered to

waiting customers will look unfamiliar to non-Asians. Among the restaurants that stand out in the hearts and palates of New Yorkers are Joe's Shanghai, Sweet-n-Tart Restaurant, Thailand, and Nha Trang, serving Vietnamese fare. The Chinatown Ice Cream Factory, a neighbourhood fixture, is known for its creamy green tea, bean curd, lychee and crystallised ginger ice creams.

Little Italy

Although Chinatown has expanded north into this area settled in the nineteenth century by Italian immigrants, Italian restaurants still line Mulberry Street and offer such classic Italian-American fare as baked ziti, fried baby octopus with marinara sauce, and veal parmesan. Glimpses of the old neighbourhood can be seen in the string of food shops on Grand Street, many still owned by the families that started them. DiPalo's Fine Foods, established in 1910, carries meat and cheeses imported from Italy and makes fresh mozzarella daily. Piemonte Ravioli Company sells

house-made pasta, tortellini and *panzotti* filled with gorgonzola cheese and porcini (cep) mushrooms. Alleva Dairy, opened in the 1890s, specialises in fresh mozzarella and ricotta, made daily, and offers other varieties of cheese as well as deli meat, olive oil, and vinegar. The Italian Food Center is stocked with a wide selection of imported products, such as oils, pastas and southern Italian specialities, and is known for its hefty hero sandwiches served on long crusty rolls.

SoHo/Nolita

Over twenty years ago, when the ground-breaking food emporium Dean & DeLuca opened on lower Broadway, Soho was a quiet neighbourhood of artists' lofts, galleries, and bistros such as Lucky Strike, Jerry's and Raoul's. Many of the lofts have become luxury flats, and the former galleries are now occupied by boutiques, but the beautiful cast-iron architecture has been preserved. Sullivan Street, one of the city's top foodie venues, represents the best of the neighbourhood, old

and new. At the north end, near Houston Street, locals stop at two neighbourhood fixtures, Joe's Dairy for fresh and smoked mozzarella and Pino Prime Meats for free-range chicken and offal. At the famed Once Upon a Tart, regulars fuel up on buttermilk currant scones and French-style pastries. Further down the street are Blue Ribbon Sushi, known for first-rate sushi and a variety of sakes, Blue Ribbon Restaurant, a hangout for restaurant chefs just off work, and Sullivan Street Bakery, which produces Italian breads and crisp-crusted pizzas.

The area east of Lafayette, known as Nolita (North of Little Italy), is occupied by small boutiques and restaurants. At its centre stands Old St. Patrick's Cathedral, consecrated in 1815. The original congregation was formed of Irish immigrants living in what was then a farming community. Today, the neighbourhood spirit is reflected in establishments such as Café Habana, serving Cuban pressed sandwiches and home-made flan, and Peasant, where hearty, seasonal Italian fare is cooked over an open fire.

Lower East Side

The area south of Houston Street and east of Bowery retains its identity as historical Jewish New York. Here are Katz's Delicatessen, the Yonah Shimmel Knishery, Kossar's Bialys, Moishe's Kosher Bake Shop, Guss' Pickles, and Russ & Daughters, which has been selling smoked fish since the early 1900s. The Lower East Side Tenement Museum on Orchard Street preserves original flats in an 1863 tenement, providing a small window into the lives of Jewish and other immigrants. With low rents attracting artists and other newcomers, the area is quickly becoming gentrified. Smart clothing boutiques and shoe shops are opening next to the old Orchard Street shopping district. The neighbourhood has also become an outpost for creative food businesses, like the acclaimed Il Laboratio del Gelato,

The Doughnut Plant, Paladar, and 71 Clinton Fresh Food. WD-50 draws patrons from all over the city who come to sample Wylie Dufresne's avant-garde preparations.

Meatpacking District

Located on the Lower West Side, abutting the north-western corner of Greenwich Village, the Meatpacking District has been a centre for the processing and distribution of food for over a century. A few of the original firms remain, among them Old Homestead, a steak-house still on its original 1868 site. Hogs and Heifers, a biker bar, draws crowds of new patrons and Florent serves hearty fare until the early-morning hours. These mainstays have been joined by recent restaurants and nightclubs. Pastis, a French bistro with outdoor seating, popular for brunch, anchors the scene on a wide-open cobblestoned corner of Little West Twelfth Street and Ninth Avenue. Every month, another establishment is opened by a chic restaurateur or chef, such as Stephen Hanson's Vento Trattoria and Jean-Georges Vongerichten's Spice Market, serving cuisine inspired by the street food of south-east Asia. The Hotel Gansevoort has also changed the landscape of the Meatpacking District immeasurably. Plans for a second hotel are in the works.

Greenwich Village

Situated on the West Side just below the Meatpacking District, and known for its tangle of streets, Greenwich Village was once a real village, a colony of artists and writers that included the poetess Edna St. Vincent Millay and playwright Eugene O'Neill. Today, its quaint, tree-lined blocks, cobbled streets, and terraced houses fetch some of the highest prices in the city. The area around New York University, south of Washington Square Park, is bustling with nightlife. The sound of jazz emanates from clubs whose patrons eat at late-night pizzerias and favourite restaurants

such as Mamoun's Falafel. The area's charming ambience and first-rate restaurants such as Babbo Ristorante e Enoteca and Blue Hill make the Village a destination for visitors from all over the city. The locals, however, prefer low-profile places such as Blue Ribbon Bakery, Corner Bistro, and Shopsin's General Store, a diner with a cult following.

To the north, Greenwich Village morphs into the West Village, location of the Spotted Pig, a British-style gastro-pub, and Barbuto, a restaurant offering contemporary seasonal fare. The West Village is also home to the famed Magnolia Bakery, where people line up for cupcakes at all hours, and The Chocolate Bar, which makes a spectacular iced "hot" chocolate.

East Village

With few exceptions, the East Village, situated between Houston and Fourteenth Streets, has generally not registered on New York's serious food scene. But in recent years, the area has changed – Tompkins Square Park is now a beautiful community resource and restaurants such as Prune, The Tasting Room, Jewel Bako, and ChikaLicious, which serves nothing but desserts, are now destination restaurants. Angelica Kitchen prepares organic vegan food to much acclaim. The area's transformations have not changed Veniero's Pasticceria, which has been owned by the same family for more than a hundred years and still draws customers seeking authentic Italian American pastries and desserts, particularly ricotta cheesecake. The hallmark of the neighbourhood is its diversity. Tibetan, Thai, Jewish deli, and Ukrainian food are all found within a five-block radius. New Yorkers pouring out of the area's many bars and nightclubs keep Veselka, a twenty-four-hour Ukrainian diner, busy all night. The East Village is home to two of the city's most popular bars: McSorley's Old Ale House, founded in 1854, which serves nothing but ale, either light or dark, and, at the opposite end of the spectrum, Angel's Share, where bartenders create cocktails using the finest alcohols and fresh juices.

Chelsea

Chelsea, just north of the Meatpacking District, once had just a few cafés and ethnic restaurants to please the locals. Kitchen Market, a tiny Mexican grocery and takeaway, had a citywide following, however, as did the Empire Diner, open all night and serving more sophisticated versions of classic diner fare. The neighbourhood food landscape began to change with the opening of Chelsea Market in 1997 (page 17) and the many art galleries. People now flock from all over town to the Maritime Hotel and its two restaurants, the basement-level Matsuri, with its elegant presentation of Japanese food, and La Bottega, a popular trattoria with an large outdoor terrace.

Gramercy Park/Flatiron District/Murray Hill

Perhaps because of their proximity to the city's largest Greenmarket, the neighbourhoods around Union Square are home to some of New York's best restaurants: City Bakery, Craft and Craftbar, Gramercy Tavern, and the pioneering Union Square Café. When Danny Meyer and Michael Romano opened Union Square Café in 1985, the once run-down neighbourhood was already starting to improve due to the influence of the Greenmarket. The gentrification has since pushed north, around the majestic, wedge-shaped Flatiron Building – completed in 1902 and considered to be the oldest still-standing skyscraper in Manhattan – and around Madison Square Park. The stretch of Lexington Avenue north-east of the park, known as Curry Hill, is a destination for New Yorkers seeking Indian restaurants and gro-ceries, most notably Kalustyan's. Many of the restaurants in this area are both kosher and vegetarian.

Midtown and the Theatre District

As New York's financial centre and home of the power lunch and the deal-closing dinner, Midtown is typified by Rockefeller Center on Fifth Avenue and is filled with legendary eating establishments, such as the Four Seasons, "21" Club, the Oyster Bar in Grand Central Station, and Smith & Wollensky, a classic steakhouse. It is also home to after-work watering holes such as P. J. Clarke's and the King Cole Bar in the St. Regis Hotel. A visit to Orso or Mario Batali's Esca, west of Times Square, before or after the theatre, is as much a part of the evening as the performance.

Hell's Kitchen

A walk up Ninth Avenue between Thirty-fourth and Forty-eighth Streets in the area known as Hell's Kitchen, passes several fine food land-marks. These include the Pozzo Pastry Shop, Empire Coffee and Tea, and Poseidon Bakery, known for the sweet and savoury fresh Greek pastries. Relative newcomers to Ninth Avenue such as the Cupcake Café and Amy's Bread marked the impending revitalisation of the neighbourhood when they opened their doors in the 1990s.

Upper West Side/Lincoln centre

The neighbourhood west of Central Park, home to landmark pre-war blocks of luxury flats, notably the Dakota and the Ansonia, had a dearth of restaurants until Tom Valenti opened Ouest in 2001 and then 'Cesca two years later. Residents are fortunate to have three of the best bagel shops in the city – Columbia Bagels, H & H Bagels, and Absolute Bagels – as well as breakfast institutions Barney Greengrass and Sarabeth's Kitchen, and the exceptional pastry shops Soutine, Levain Bakery, and Margot Patisserie. Added to this abundance are three of the most ven-erated food stores in the city: Zabar's, Fairway, and Gourmet Garage. For patrons attending the theatre, opera or concerts at Lincoln Center to the south, a late-night dinner at Café des Artistes or Café Luxembourg is a ritual. At the south end of the neighbourhood, near Central Park, stands Trump Tower, housing the four-star Jean Georges. Across the reno-vated Columbus Circle stands the Time Warner Center, a complex containing the restaurants run by celebrated chefs from all over the United States, including Californian Thomas Keller's Per Se.

East Side/Upper East Side

Millionnaires' mansions once stood east of Central Park, from Fifty-Ninth Street into the Nineties. One of the few remaining mansions now houses the Frick Collection of Old Masters. Just to the north, the Metropolitan Museum of Art, right on Central Park, is the focal point of Museum Mile, which contains the Jewish Museum and the Solomon R. Guggenheim Museum. Stylishness still defines Fifth, Madison, and Park Avenues, where posh shops such as Lobel's Prime Meats, Rosenthal Wine Merchant, and Sherry-Lehmann, another wine shop, are legendary for their high-quality products and lofty prices. Elegance characterises East Side eateries such as Daniel, Aureole, Payard Patisserie

and Bistro, and Bemelmans Bar at the Carlyle Hotel. Eli Zabar's Vinegar Factory is a destination for shoppers seeking an extensive selection of gourmet foods, as well as Zabar's renowned breads. Chocoholics are drawn to La Maison du Chocolat, selling French confectionery and hot chocolate drinks.

The area between the high Seventies and Eighties, known as Yorkville, was once a German and Hungarian enclave. This heritage is preserved in a few fine butchers' such as Yorkville Meat Emporium, Ottomanelli Brothers Market, and Schatzie's Prime Meats. At Orwasher's Bakery, the Orwasher family has been making rye bread from the same recipe – and using the same leaven starter – for almost a hundred years.

Harlem

The Dutch who first settled here in the early 1600s named the area after Haarlem in the Netherlands. Harlem has attracted various waves of immigrants over the centuries, and by the late 1800s it was a mecca for wealthy Manhattanites who lined the streets with brownstones and townhouses, many of which have since been declared landmarks. African-Americans leaving the South in the early 1900s gravitated to Harlem, bringing about an efflorescence of artistic culture and social philosophy in the 1920s and 1930s known as the Harlem Renaissance. The Apollo theatre, a survivor of that time, still anchors Central Harlem. In this area north of Central Park from Fifth Avenue west to St. Nicolas, soul food rules, and the dining options are many, including the established M & G Diner and Better Crust Bakery, hailed for its apple, pecan and sweet potato pies, and newcomer Miss Mamie's Spoonbread Too. Sylvia's Soul Food is world-famous, Sylvia Woods having been dubbed "The Queen of Soul Food" by *New York Magazine*. In East Harlem, which lies east of Fifth Avenue, Patsy's Pizzeria and Rao's are remnants of what was once an Italian neighbourhood. Today the area, also known as Spanish Harlem or El Barrio, is home to various Hispanic populations and to many Puerto Rican and Mexican groceries. La Hacienda specialises in traditional Mexican fare and La Fonda Boricua is known for homespun Puerto Rican dishes such as yellow rice, black beans and stews.

The Bronx

North of Manhattan lies the only borough not separated from Manhattan by water. The Bronx is most famous as home of the world-class zoo and Yankee Stadium. Near the stadium is F & J Pine Restaurant, a favourite post-game dinner spot. One of the most culturally interesting areas of the Bronx is Belmont, sometimes referred to as the Little Italy of the Bronx for the dominant Sicilian population that settled there in the nineteenth century. This community's epicentre is the Arthur Avenue Retail Market, a block-long row of shops selling fruit and vegetables, delicatessen, and cheeses, surrounded by other Italian shops and restaurants (page 21). Loaded down with goods, hungry shoppers stop for a slice of pizza at Full Moon Pizza or

a big plate of spaghetti and meatballs at Mario's. A trip to City Island, a historic seaport, would be incomplete without a visit to the Lobster Box, a fixture since the mid-1940s, or Johnny's Famous Reef, a casual eatery offering fried seafood, outdoor seating, and a view of Long Island Sound – a totally unexpected New York dining experience.

Brooklyn

The range of thriving ethnic communities in Brooklyn is as diverse as in any borough, from the Russian enclave in Brighton Beach to the Hasidic community of Williamsburg. Brooklyn is also home to yet another Little Italy, the neighbourhood known as Bensonhurst. In 1915, Italian immigrants migrated to what was then farmland after the completion of the Fourth Avenue train line from Manhattan. Today, Eighteenth Avenue maintains its community feel, with outdoor fruit and vegetable markets and small family-run stores such as Bari Pork Store, Trunzo Bros., and Villabate Pasticceria, which specialises in Sicilian pastries, including ricotta-filled cannoli and sanguinaccio.

In Sunset Park, Bat Dai Do, which translates as "Eighth Avenue" and also means "road to prosperity" in Cantonese, has quickly become New York City's second largest Chinatown, settled primarily by Cantonese immigrants from Hong Kong. The area's diversity can be seen in a Vietnamese sandwich shop called Ba Xuyjen, El Tepeyac Mini-Mart, specialising in Mexican and Ecuadorean foods, and the Turkish Birlik Food Market. At the far end of this large borough lies Coney Island, the world-famous amusement park where hot dogs were invented and are still sold near the beachside boardwalk (promenade), of which the veteran is Nathan's Famous.

Brooklyn's recent popularity is reflected in the opening of trendy restaurants including Blue Ribbon in Park Slope and Relish and Oznot's Dish in Williamsburg, and gourmet shops such as former chef Jacques Torres' Chocolate in Dumbo (Down Under the Manhattan Brooklyn Overpass).

Queens

The largest of the five boroughs and home to both La Guardia and JFK airports, Queens is the gateway to New York and the most ethnically diverse area in the United States. An estimated 138 languages are spoken here, including Chinese, Korean, Italian, Greek, Russian, and French. Flushing, near Shea Stadium, has become predominantly Asian. Vendors sell fried noodles and cafés such as Relax Tea House specialise in Chinese pastries and bubble tea, a mixture of tea, milk and large tapioca pearls. Asian restaurants range from Green Papaya Thai Cuisine and the Taiwanese Laifood to Pho Vietnamese Restaurant and Penang, serving Malaysian food. The Greek population that once dominated Astoria now shares the territory with immigrants from Thailand, North Africa and Yugoslavia, but institutions such as Christos Hasapo-Taverna, a Greek steakhouse, Telly's Taverna, serving seafood and Titan Foods, a grocery, still offer authentic Greek cuisine.

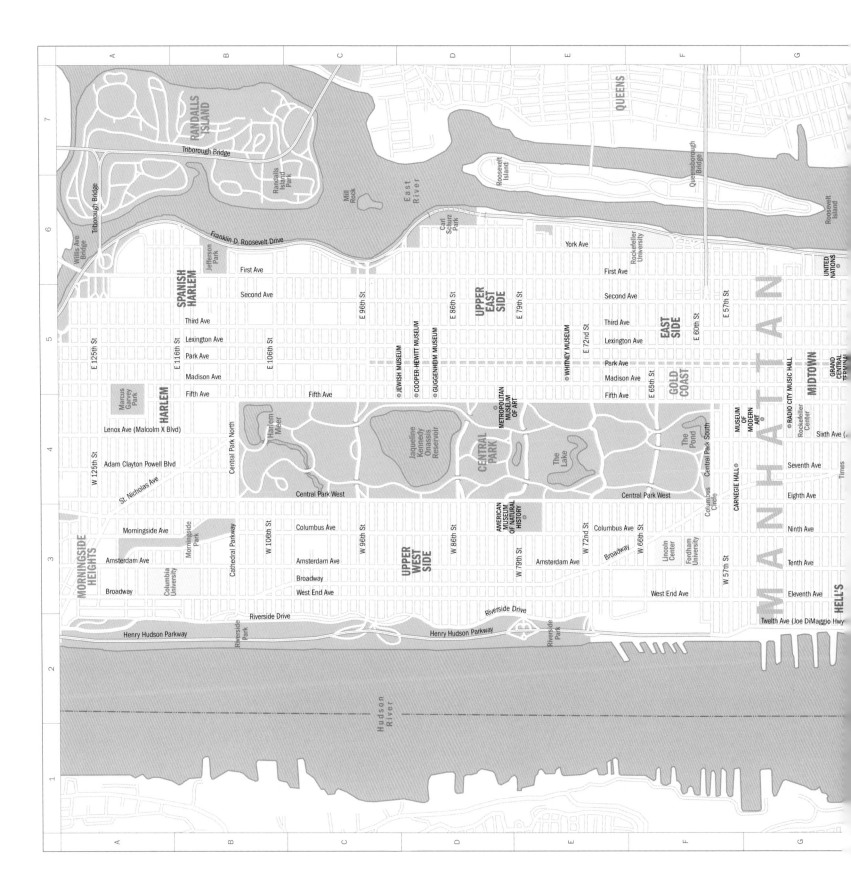

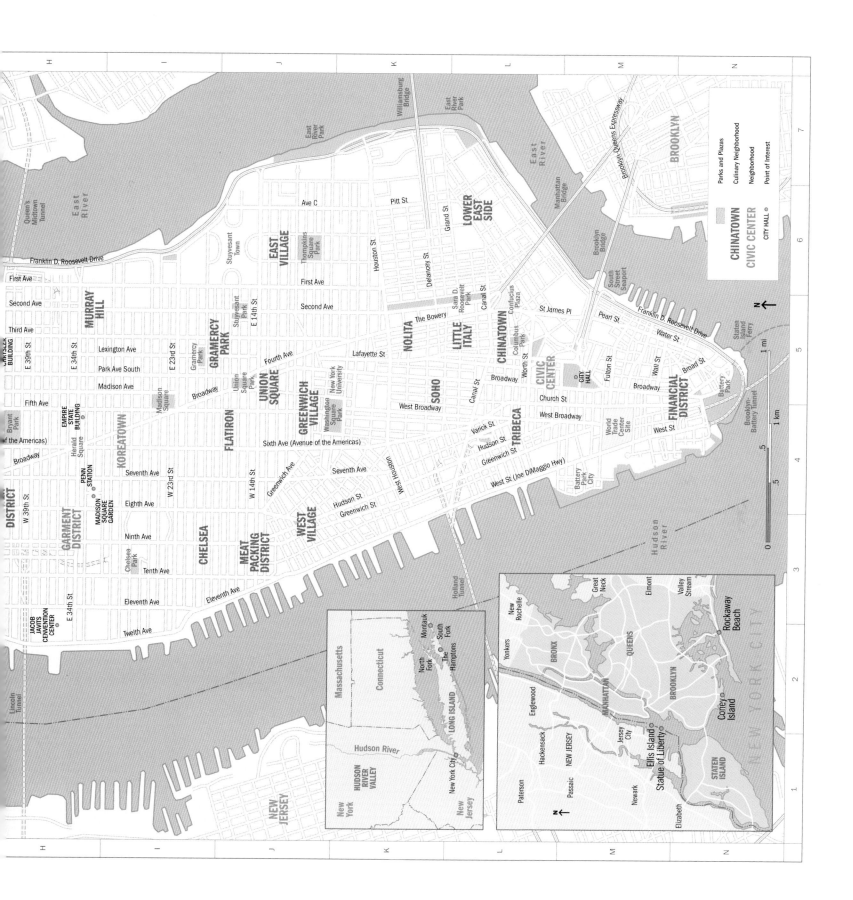

Best of **NEW YORK**

In the twenty years since Eli Zabar began turning out crusty, chewy, European-style loaves, New Yorkers have developed high standards for baked goods, demanding freshness and top quality. They seek out small, specialist bakeries for everything from *ciabatta* and challah to tarts and cupcakes.

BAKERIES AND BAGEL SHOPS

New York's artisanal bread movement owes its explosive growth over the last two decades to several factors. One was an accident. In 1987, Eli Zabar discovered a coal-fired brick oven in the basement at E.A.T., his smart delicatessen on the Upper East Side. Having studied under the late Lionel Poilâne, of the renowned Parisian boulangerie, he had been baking bread in a pizza oven for a few years. He took the discovery of the oven as an omen and started a full-scale bakery operation called Eli's Bread.

Zabar's first signature loaf was the long, skinny *ficelle,* and for the next year, he gave most of the bread away. Business finally began to develop after a few notable chefs and restaurateurs began using Eli's Bread almost exclusively. As New Yorkers' tastes grew more sophisticated, European-style

bread became the standard. Eli's selection expanded to more than twelve different types of dough and even more variations, and other bread bakers, such as Amy's Bread, Sullivan Street Bakery, and Tom Cat Bakery, soon entered the scene.

Today, New Yorkers are such connoisseurs that a loaf of bread – just like a cupcake, a bagel or a croissant – is considered only as good as the bakery in which it was made. Every baker produces a signature item that reflects his or her style. *Ciabatta* from Sullivan Street Bakery, semolina-raisin loaf from Amy's Bread, wholemeal bread from Tom Cat Bakery, tarts from City Bakery, and croissants from Ceci-Cela.

New York's immigrant population brought their baking traditions with them, and many of those early bakeries still thrive today. On the

quickly gentrifying Lower East Side, challah, *babka,* bagels and bialys are still made using the same methods as in the "old country". Thin-crusted Italian loaves are pulled out of ancient brick ovens in Italian enclaves from Little Italy in Manhattan to Arthur Avenue in the Bronx to Bensonhurst in Brooklyn.

Loaves of freshly baked bread are sold at New York's priciest supermarkets, and good bagel-sellers can be found in most neighbourhoods. But for pastries, it would not be unusual for a New Yorker to go across town to fill a baklava craving at Poseidon Bakery, to head downtown to buy a ricotta cheesecake from Veneiro's Pasticceria for a dinner party or to stop at Magnolia Bakery, Buttercup Bake Shop, or Cupcake Café to pick up a dozen cupcakes for a birthday party.

For a bagel aficionado, hand-rolled bagels are the only acceptable kind.

Best eaten shortly after they are made, bagels are turned out by the thousands each day at the city's bagelries. Expert bagel-makers say there is no such thing as a definitive recipe. The preparation changes daily, depending on the temperature and humidity. Adjusting the recipe requires knowing how the dough should feel and look at each stage of the process.

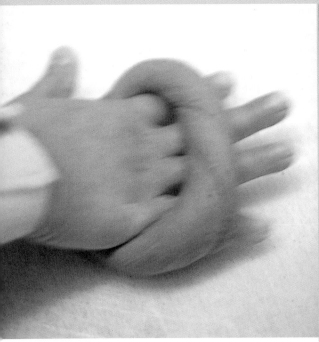

Cream Cheese and Bagels

Significant enough as the main ingredient in New York cheesecake, cream cheese is perhaps valued even more on bagels. New Yorkers ask for a "shmear", from a Yiddish term meaning a little cheese smeared on the cut sides of a halved bagel. Bagel shops offer many varieties of cream cheese, including chive and lox (smoked salmon), the most popular. Of the handful of artisanal cream cheeses, Ben's is considered the best.

Bagel Toppings

At one time, the only types of bagels produced were plain and those topped with salt, sesame seeds and poppyseeds. As bagel shops proliferated outside the city as well as in the five boroughs, variations on the bagel have multiplied. Purists now willingly acknowledge egg, rye, onion, garlic, pumpernickel and cinnamon-raisin bagels. There are also "everything bagels", topped with a mixture of salt, seeds, onion and garlic. Nine-grain bagels are the most recent acceptable addition to the roster.

Although traditionalists have shown they have an open mind, it is possible to go too far. Authentic New York bagel shops do not make bagels containing sun-dried tomatoes, jalapeño chillies, blueberries, chocolate chips or pesto. Perhaps surprisingly, mini bagels are welcomed. Offered at well-known shops like Absolute Bagel on the Upper West Side, these bagels are close to the original size of bagels made a century ago. Back then, a bagel weighed about 90 grams (3 oz), about half of what the average bagel weighs today.

Making Bagels

MIXING THE DOUGH Bagels start with a simple mixture of flour, salt, fresh yeast, water, and barley malt, which is preferred over sugar.

SHAPING THE DOUGH Bakers at the best shops insist on forming the dough traditionally – by hand rather than by machine. The dough is first cut into small rectangles. Each is rolled into a tube and is then shaped into a ring.

BOILING THE BAGELS Before they are baked, bagels are boiled, a process known as kettling,

named for the large iron pots used in bagelries. The moisture absorbed by the dough gives the finished bagels a moist, almost cakey quality. The bagels are removed from the boiling water when they float to the top, after about 60 seconds. The bagels are immediately dipped into buckets containing the appropriate topping ingredients.

BAKING THE BAGELS Within minutes after coming out of the kettle, bagels are transferred to a 260°C (500°F) oven and baked until golden brown.

RICOTTA CHEESECAKE

CUPCAKES

BABKA

CANNOLI

DOUGHNUTS

BAKLAVA

LEMON TARTLETS

CROISSANTS

CUPCAKES

Simple vanilla and chocolate, with a swirl of pastel-tinted frosting, are the most common cupcakes. Bakers put their signature on the little cakes by topping them with glaze, icing, or sprinkles, or by baking them in French paper baking cups.

BAKLAVA

To make this intensely sweet Greek pastry, tissue-thin sheets of phyllo are brushed with clarified butter and layered with chopped nuts, baked, and then drizzled with honey syrup.

LEMON TARTLETS

French-style tarts and tartlets are served in cafés and restaurants as elegant alternatives to American pie. Lemon-filled tartlets, made with a vanilla or chocolate pastry case, are a winter favourite. Summer tart fillings include blueberry-coconut and plum-almond.

RICOTTA CHEESECAKE

This dense cake with a lemony flavour and crumbly texture is a mainstay of Sicilian bakeries. The cookie crust is filled with a mixture of ricotta, cream cheese, eggs, and lemon zest.

CANNOLI

Fried pastry cases stuffed with what Italian New Yorkers call "cannoli cream", a mixture of ricotta cheese and double cream, can be seen in the windows of bakeries in any Italian neighbourhood. Variations on the Sicilian dessert include dipping the tube-shaped shells in chocolate, stuffing them with flavoured creams such as almond, or adding ingredients like mini chocolate chips or candied citrus to the filling. Villabate Pasticceria in Brooklyn makes only one type of cannoli: the original, filled with imported sheep's milk ricotta.

DOUGHNUTS

The popularity of crullers, jelly-filled doughnuts, and other standard versions has never waned. But a new kind of doughnut arrived in 1994, when The Donut Plant in the Lower East Side began turning out fluffy glazed doughnuts using such high-end ingredients as Valrhona chocolate and seasonal fresh fruit.

CROISSANTS

The perfect Parisian croissants, from Ceci-Cela, are buttery with a thin, crisp exterior and a flaky interior. In addition to classic plain versions, the bakery makes chocolate, almond, and chocolate-almond croissants.

CHALLAH

RYE BREAD

BAGEL

KNISH

BIALY

PECAN RAISIN BREAD

BABKA AND CHALLAH

Babka is a dense, rich, Polish coffee cake usually eaten for dessert or breakfast. Challah is a golden, egg-enriched yeast bread often shaped by braiding the dough. The loaves are traditionally eaten on Jewish Sabbath and at certain holidays.

PECAN RAISIN BREAD

Inspired by the raisin-pumpernickel bread in many Jewish bakeries, Eli Zabar created this signature bread. Made from organic stone-ground white flour, the bread is dense with both ground pecans and chopped pecans. Many artisanal bakers make a similar version.

RYE BREAD

Good rye makes the difference between a great deli sandwich and a disappointing one. Orwasher's Bakery specialises in this traditional eastern European bread. Abram Orwasher, who runs the business his grandfather started, says that the sourdough culture is the key to good rye. He employs the same culture used when the bakery opened in 1916. The bakery sells traditional rye, which is made with a combination of rye and wheat flours, either with or without caraway seeds. It also makes corn rye, a traditional rye that uses a higher ratio of rye flour to wheat flour.

KNISH

This Jewish pastry from eastern Europe is made with a thin, light dough filled with spinach, meat, or, most commonly, a mixture of mashed potato and onion. The best knishes come from old shops that specialise in them, such as Yonah Schimmel Knishery, Mrs. Stahl's Knishes, and Knish Nosh's Knishes.

BIALY

Named for the Polish city of Bialystok, where it originated, the bialy is a Jewish bread that, unlike a bagel, is not boiled, but is sprinkled before baking with sautéed onions, and lacks a hole.

BAGEL

The Jewish doughnut-shaped yeast bread originated in Europe in the seventeenth century and reached its zenith in the hands of New York bakers. Authentic bagels, like those from Ess-a-Bagel, are rolled by hand and quickly boiled before being baked, giving them a shiny surface and a characteristic dense, chewy interior. Purists who once preferred unadorned bagels have come to embrace a variety of toppings. Among the acceptable ones are sesame seeds, poppy seeds, salt, and onions.

Jewish and Italian delicatessens offer glimpses into the experiences and traditions of the city's early immigrants. Customers eagerly line up at deli counters to order a pastrami sandwich on rye or a hero brimming with meat and all the extras.

DELICATESSENS

The New York delicatessen dates back to the nineteenth century, when Jewish immigrants began making pastrami (salt beef) as a way of preserving meat. The beef was cured for twenty-one days in a brine containing coriander, pepper, garlic and cloves. Then it was hickory-smoked for eight hours, trimmed and, finally, steamed until succulent and tender. The process proved too labour-intensive for home cooks, who welcomed the delis that sprang up in Jewish neighbourhoods to sell pastrami. By the 1930s, over five thousand delis throughout the city specialised in custom-cured pastrami. These establishments typically had only a few counter seats and were also known for their frankfurters, knishes, rye bread and pickled cucumber.

According to Jewish dietary law, the preparation of meat and dairy foods must be kept separate, requiring separate cutlery and crockery. Thus separate kosher deli restaurants and kosher dairy restaurants were established to cater to the needs of religious Jews. Delis became known for their ample pastrami, corned beef and brisket sandwiches served with coleslaw and French fries and for other meat items, such as potroast beef flanken and cabbage stuffed with minced beef and rice. Dairies, in contrast, served Jewish foods containing milk and milk-based products. The fifty-year-old Diamond Dairy Restaurant, its long counter and half-dozen tables on the glassed-in second floor of the New York Diamond Exchange, is the only dairy left in Manhattan and one of the few in the city. In the dairy tradition, the restaurant is known for its cheese blintzes (cheese-filled pancakes) and kugel (baked *lokshen* (noodle) pudding).

The number of delis has dwindled to a mere scattering in each borough. Many of them are new and cater to tourists seeking a New York deli experience. The pastrami now comes from the few traditional producers that remain in Brooklyn and the Bronx. Revered delis, such as Katz's Delicatessen and Carnegie Deli in Manhattan and Ben's Best in Queens, still take great pride in offering traditional and succulent pastrami, made to their specifications, and always sliced to order.

Second Avenue Deli, located for fifty years in an area of the East Village once known as the Jewish Rialto for its concentration of Yiddish theatres, and Ben's Best, established in 1945 in Rego Park, are true kosher delis. The city's other delis, however, are "kosher style". Such kosher-style delis as Carnegie Deli, Katz's Delicatessen and Stage Deli retain

From sandwiches to cheesecake, deli food is beloved for its ample portions.

the essence of the Jewish eating experience in America, while also offering dairy items such as New York cheesecake and egg creams (condensed milk and soda water). Another favourite is the Reuben sandwich, grilled corned beef with Swiss cheese and Russian dressing, named after the deli where it was supposedly invented.

Upon entering a deli, diners encounter salamis and other meats hanging overhead, and glass cases filled with chopped liver, whitefish salad, spinach and potato knishes, lox and apple strudel. Along the walls are stacks of rye bread loaves, jars of Fox's U-Bet

Houston Street, a reminder of the deli's past slogan: "Send a salami to your boy in the army". Patrons take a number upon entering and line up along the counter, where they watch juicy meat being sliced by hand. After ordering, customers are given a slice to taste before their sandwiches are made. Many of the waiters have been there as long as fifty years. Their friendly gruffness is really an act; they might sit down later and join your party.

A sandwich that rivals those in Jewish delis in heft and sentiment is the Italian hero. Food writer Clementine Paddleford named it in 1936 after remarking, "You'd have to be a

What all of these delicatessens have in common is a sense of bounty, that more is definitely more. The pastrami sandwiches are so huge that they barely fit in the mouth.

Chocolate Flavour Syrup, cases of Dr. Brown's Cel-Ray Tonic, boxes of kosher salt – all available for purchase and reflecting the days when delis also functioned as grocery stores with the convenience of being open on Sundays. Complimentary plates of sweet-and-sour and new green pickled cucumbers are on every table. The pastrami sandwiches are so huge that they barely fit in the mouth.

Although many New Yorkers dismiss it as a tourist destination, Carnegie Deli, located in the Theatre District since 1937, offers its own style of authenticity. The walls are lined with celebrity photographs and sandwiches weigh in at a whopping 450 grams (one pound) each, qualifying them as the biggest in the city. The sandwiches carry names like "The Woody Allen", "Fifty Ways to Love Your Liver", and "Tongue's for the Memory". Surly waiters in black tie make out-of-towners feel they are experiencing a true New York phenomenon.

A trip to Katz's, a Lower East Side institution since 1888, is a step back in time. Salamis hang in the large windows along

hero to finish one". The foundation is a crusty white roll whose soft interior is scooped out to hold copious amounts of sliced meat and cheese, plus pepperoncini, roasted sweet peppers or sun-dried tomatoes. The meat is salami, prosciutto, capicolla, mortadella, or turkey, and the cheese is fresh or smoked mozzarella or provolone. The sandwich is often finished with a drizzle of olive oil and red wine vinegar and salt and pepper.

Heros are made to order on crusty rolls at Faicco's Pork Store, a cheery shop on Bleecker Street in the West Village, where one side is lined with imported canned goods, the other with a butcher case and a deli case filled with olives, marinated mushrooms, and capsicums. At the Italian Food Center on Grand Street, banners hanging over a counter that runs the length of the shop advertise sandwich specials – "The New Yorker", "The Little Italy" – each weighing over 450 grams. Olive oil, house-made mozzarella, and anchovies are among the large selection of foods offered, a relic of Little Italy's past.

In its abundance, availability, and quality, the fare sold on city streets is considered a respectable option to a sit-down meal. New Yorkers, famously in a hurry, can enjoy foods ranging from the simplest snacks to gourmet lunches by celebrity chefs.

STREET FOOD

Much of life in New York takes place on the streets. Walking is considered a respectable means of transport, and the food sold from quilted stainless-steel carts, insulated kiosks, and tiny shop windows fuels New Yorkers as they go to and from work, grab lunch or pause for a snack.

Eating food sold from street vendors has been part of the city's streetscape since its beginning, and peddling food on the street has always proved a viable means for recently arrived immigrants to earn a living. The overheads are minimal, and the stream of customers steady. After the Potato Famine of the mid-1800s, young Irish newcomers sold potatoes roasted over open fires. In the 1880s, Chinese immigrants added rock candy to the city's movable feast. Italian immigrants sold sausage and capsicums and *zeppole,*

fried dough sprinkled with icing sugar, from pavement stands, a tradition that continues on Arthur Avenue in the Bronx and at summer street fairs like Little Italy's Feast of San Gennaro. In the early 1900s, vendors on the Lower East Side offered hot dogs with sauerkraut for a nickel. Although selling street food is now more regulated and permits are required, immigrants still dominate the trade.

In pockets throughout the five boroughs, the fare sold on the street still reflects the culture of the neighbourhood. On Canal Street in Chinatown, crowds five deep gather around vendors selling spring onion pancakes, roast duck, pleated dumplings and stir-fried noodles. Further south, near Wall Street, vendors fry bacon and eggs for a desk-bound clientele. In the Eastern European enclave of Brighton Beach, borscht is ladled from pavement

stands. Tamales, empanadas, tacos, and other Mexican and Central American fare reign in Brooklyn's Red Hook neighbourhood.

Although street food has become standardised over the years, there is the occasional original: a popcorn vendor on Delancey Street, a seller of oversized stuffed baked potatoes in Midtown, a window on Ninth Avenue in the East Village offering *okonomiyaki,* Japanese fried vegetable pancakes. Street food has also gone fancy. Adam Perry Lang, of Daisy May's BBQ U.S.A., has stalls in Midtown and on Wall Street that specialise in American chili and pulled-pork sandwiches. Danny Meyer, of Union Square Café and Gramercy Tavern, opened the Shake Shack in Madison Square Park, which sells hot dogs, hamburgers, and "old-fashioned frozen custard".

Street food has two highly desirable qualities: it's fast and it's economical.

COFFEE AND A ROLL

Breakfast on the go – a cup of coffee, along with a plain roll, sliced in half and slathered with butter – was a ritual long before the chain coffee shops came along. No matter what corner deli or barrow the coffee comes from, it is poured into an iconic blue-and-white paper cup emblazoned with a depiction of the Acropolis. There is a language for ordering coffee from these stands: black (no milk, no sugar), dark (a little cream), light (lots of cream), and regular (cream and the sugar from two packets).

FRUIT

Sold from large wooden tables, often shaded by an umbrella, fruit provides a healthy, inexpensive breakfast or snack. Vendors stand behind large scales weighing each customer's selection from the flats of berries and piles of apples, oranges, bananas and bunches of grapes. In Harlem in the summer, trucks piled sky-high with water-melons park on 125th Street and sell them right off the truck. In Chinatown, the vendors' stands sell exotic favourites such as lychees and mangoes.

ROASTED NUTS

The unmistakable aroma of chest-nuts roasting over a coal brazier marks the winter festive season on Fifth Avenue. Plucked from the coals, the hot chestnuts are placed in large paper cones. Peeling the charred skins is all part of the experience of eating the buttery flesh inside. The sweet smell of honey-roasted nuts, a selection of peanuts, almonds, and cashews, combined with shards of coconut flesh, beckons year-round from barrows throughout the city.

HOT DOGS AND SAUSAGES

Nathan's Famous in Coney Island, true to its name, made hot dogs famous and still serves them from a window at the original Brooklyn location. The typical boiled hot dog from a street vendor is accom-panied by sauerkraut, yellow mus-tard, onions stewed with tomatoes and perhaps a pickled cucumber relish. The Hallo Berlin pushcart on Fifth Avenue offers an array of wursts that cater to New Yorkers' increasingly discerning tastes. Long queues are proof that a Gray's Papaya hot dog, at various Manhattan locations, is a favourite.

SOFT PRETZELS

NOODLES

FALAFEL

SOFT PRETZELS

Although the oversized soft pretzel is a Philadelphia invention, New York still claims some of the credit. Sold on the streets of New York as early as the 1920s, it is one of the few street-foods of yesteryear that is still offered from barrows today. The same vendors who serve hot dogs sell the pretzels, keeping them warm over rock salt, some of which sticks to their shiny surface. Once ordered, vendors place a pretzel on a sheet of aluminium foil and offer to squeeze brown mustard on top.

SOUP

Satisfying and healthy, soup is an increasingly popular lunchtime meal sold from shop windows and small kiosks. At Al Yeganeh's Soup Kitchen International in Midtown, the proprietor ladles up ten varieties, including classics such as lentil soup, spicy chilli and lobster bisque, and his own inventions, such as Greek moussaka soup. Another popular soup kiosk is a roofed extension on the SoHo pub Finelli's. The stand sells ten soups each day, including Cuban black bean, corn chowder and chilled tomato gazpacho.

NOODLES

Any language barrier to ordering food in a Chinatown restaurant is easily overcome when buying from a street vendor. As pedestrians inch their way along the crowded pavements, they can see what is on offer and merely point to what they want. Barrows selling noodles generally offer three types: *mai fun,* rice vermicelli fried with eggs and cabbage; *lo mein,* spaghetti-shaped egg noodles tossed with vegetables and other stir-fried ingredients; and *cheung fun,* steamed rice noodle rolls.

FALAFEL

Of all the cuisines of recent immigrant populations, Middle Eastern food has wholeheartedly won over the appetites of New Yorkers. This can be measured, in part, by the number of street vendors selling gyros (döner kebab) and falafel, the spicy cumin-scented chick-pea balls that are deep-fried, then stuffed into pitta bread along with lettuce, tomatoes, onions and chilli sauce. Moshe's Falafel in Midtown is legendary for making the best falafel, deep-fried to order.

New York–style pizza has become legendary well beyond the city. The dough is prepared daily and the simple toppings rely on the freshest ingredients. The crisp, blistered crust comes from baking the assembled pizza at a high temperature in a coal-fired oven.

PIZZA

The roots of New York pizza, affectionately known as pizza pie, can be traced to the 1890s, when Italian grocers began using their bread ovens and bread dough to make Neapolitan-style pizzas dressed with tomato sauce and mozzarella cheese. By all accounts, Gennaro Lombardi, who began selling the pies from his grocery store in Little Italy in the early 1900s, owned the city's first pizza parlour. The bakers behind the pizzerias began their careers at Lombardi's store. Anthony "Totonno" Pero went on to open Totonno Pizzeria Napoletano in Coney Island in 1924. Five years later, John Sasso established John's Pizzeria in Greenwich Village. Pascale Lancieri started Patsy's Pizzeria in East Harlem in 1933.

What makes the pies at these pizzerias and a handful of others exceptional is largely the quality of the ingredients that go into them, the care with which the pizzas are made, and the way that they are baked. The San Marzano tomato, an Italian Roma tomato prized for its sweetness, is the variety of choice for the sauce. The mozzarella is hand-made, often in the neighbourhood.

Of crucial importance is the coal-fired brick oven in which the pizzas are baked. Only a finite number of these ovens are in existence today, and it is illegal to build new ones, so new pizzerias wishing to make pizzas the old-fashioned way must find locations with pre-existing ovens. The fire in the ovens is never allowed to go out, and is stoked each morning with more coal, until, by the time the pizzeria opens, the oven has reached a steady temperature of 455°C (850°F). A pizza is slid into the oven and, just minutes later, emerges piping hot with a crust that is crisp but still pliant and evenly marked on the bottom with charred blisters.

There is, in fact, another New York pizza. Sicilian-style pizza may not be as popular, but it has its fans. This thick, puffy bread, fragrant with olive oil, is baked in a Swiss roll tin and then cut into rectangles. It is usually offered along with variations on the traditional slice.

In the last decade, New Yorkers have gained a renewed appreciation for authentic New York pizza and often debate who makes the best. This passion for pizza has spawned new pizzerias, all offshoots of the reigning New York pizza families and all using coal-fired ovens. John's now has many locations in Manhattan, Totonno has a pizzeria on the Upper West Side and Grimaldi's has a first-rate pizza place in Brooklyn.

When it comes to New York pizza, tradition, not innovation, is what counts.

Making pizza is a craft that requires years of practise. Apprentice pizza-makers work in the prep kitchen for months before they are allowed to perform the tasks of one of the four frontline positions: expanding the dough and spreading the sauce on top, arranging the cheese and other toppings, baking the pizza in a coal-fired brick oven, and slicing the hot pizza.

Folding a New York Slice

When in need of a quick bite, New Yorkers stop for a hot slice of pizza. By-the-slice pizza parlours throughout the city often have tables for standing only. The slice is warmed in the oven before being placed on a plate and slid over the counter to a hungry customer. A New Yorker typically folds the slice lengthways from the tip, so the toppings are contained inside. Folding the large, unwieldy slice makes it easier to manage – and easier to eat on the run.

Pizza Toppings

In New York, pizza is not a platform for experimentation. Ingredients that pass for toppings in other cities, such as barbecue sauce or pineapple, are met with head-shaking bewilderment. New York pizza is plain, which means topped with tomato sauce and fresh mozzarella. Or it is adorned with traditional Italian toppings including pepperoni, sweet sausage, meatballs, sweet peppers, onions, mushrooms and/or anchovies.

The most likely style to puzzle out-of-towners is white pizza, *pizza bianca*. White pizza is just what it sounds like. It is topped with mozzarella, ricotta and grated romano cheese. Lombardi's in Little Italy is known for its clam pie, a tradition from New Haven, Connecticut, made with freshly-shelled clams, garlic and oregano. Two Boots, with locations in Manhattan and Brooklyn, is known for its pioneering cornmeal crust. The toppings, which are certainly not accepted by pizza traditionalists, include barbecued prawns, crayfish, andouille sausage, jalapeño chillies and spicy buffalo (chicken) wings.

Making Pizza

MAKING THE DOUGH Prepared daily, the dough uses fresh yeast and high-gluten flour. After being kneaded, it is rubbed with olive oil and left to rise.

OPENING THE DOUGH This expression refers to the process of turning a ball of dough into a large, thin round. Tossing the spinning round into the air is considered showmanship. More traditional methods include pulling the edges out with both hands or passing the dough back and forth from one hand to the other. The round should have no thick spots and no thin areas or holes.

TOPPING THE PIZZA At some pizzerias, fresh mozzarella slices are placed on the round, and the sauce is ladled over them. Elsewhere, the sauce goes on first, followed by the cheese. Other traditional toppings are then scattered on top.

BAKING THE PIZZA A "stick man" wielding a long wooden peel deftly slides the pizza into a coal-fired oven without dislodging the toppings. The pizza needs only 3 minutes in the hot oven, during which time it is rotated every 30 seconds for even baking.

Meeting for a cocktail is a ritual form of entertainment in New York. At trendy watering holes or neighbourhood drinking dens, casual bistros or elegant hotel bars, New Yorkers like to get together after work or party well into the early-morning hours.

BARS AND COCKTAILS

New York's bar scene is as old as the city itself. The earliest settlers frequented taverns opened by the Dutch in the 1600s. Public houses arrived with the Irish immigrants two centuries later. But New York's reputation as a serious bar town was not cemented until the 1920s, with the proliferation of speakeasies during the Prohibition era. Two are still thriving today: the "21" Club in Midtown and Chumley's in Greenwich Village.

The city's bar scene is inextricably tied to its literary scene. Many famous writers, among them Chumley's regulars, F. Scott Fitzgerald and Jack Kerouac, were also legendary drinkers. A plaque marks the spot where poet Dylan Thomas collapsed at the White Horse Tavern, another famous Greenwich Village watering hole. The renowned Algonquin Round Table at the Algonquin Hotel included

Dorothy Parker and A. L. Mencken. Mencken, quotable on many subjects, described the martini as "the only American invention as perfect as a sonnet".

In an effort to start new trends, some bars are based on a theme. Pravda in SoHo, specialising in vodka, pours brands from around the world. Sakagura in Midtown is devoted to sake and carries dozens of varieties. The bars at bistros like Balthazar in SoHo and Pastis in Greenwich Village invite customers to drink as the French do, by enjoying an aperitif such as a Champagne cocktail before dinner. New Yorkers also like authenticity and patina, so many of the most popular bars are the oldest: Pete's Tavern, Ear Inn, and P. J. Clarke's.

Some of the city's liveliest bars are in the lobbies of hip hotels such as hotelier Ian Schrager's Hudson and Royalton in Midtown.

Downtown, the Mercer Hotel in Soho and the Maritime Hotel in Chelsea attract crowds of New Yorkers and out-of-towners day and night. The elegant hotel bars on the East Side have a dedicated clientele. The Oak Bar and the Oyster Bar at the Plaza Hotel, Bemelmans Bar in the Carlyle Hotel, and the King Cole Bar in the St. Regis Hotel – where the Bloody Mary got its name – evoke a sophistication and glamour associated with an earlier era.

New Yorkers take their cocktails seriously, and thankfully so do many of the city's bartenders. Bars such as Milk and Honey, Angel's Share, and Temple Bar are known for using house-squeezed juices, fresh garnishes and top brands of spirits. Whatever their current preference, New Yorkers eagerly await the next drink that might become as iconic as the Manhattan or the cosmopolitan.

From martinis to mojitos, New York's vibrant bar scene is as diverse as the city.

INFUSED VODKA

MOJITO

MANHATTAN

GIBSON

CLASSIC MARTINI

CLASSIC MARTINI

The vodka martini has its adherents, but the gin martini, on the rocks or strained into a chilled martini glass and garnished with green olives or a lemon twist, is the classic. According to legend, the cocktail debuted in the late 1800s at the Occidental Hotel in San Francisco. The name it now goes by may have come from the vermouth company, Martini and Rossi. The drink came into its own in New York, where President Franklin D. Roosevelt toasted the end of Prohibition in 1933 with a dirty martini – a martini with a splash of olive brine.

INFUSED VODKA

In the early 1990s, infused vodka first appeared in Manhattan. Bars made their own flavoured spirits by pouring vodka into large glass jugs containing fruit such as pineapple slices or whole berries. Responding to the trend, manufacturers began producing their own infused vodkas. One bar that continues the tradition is Pravda, in SoHo, which carries a selection of vodkas from around the world, but the house specialities are the custom infusions, including blackberry, cherry, pineapple, coconut, and ginger and the cocktails made with them.

MANHATTAN

In 1874, Sir Winston Churchill's mother, Lady Randolph Churchill, hosted a party at the Manhattan Club to celebrate the election of New York Governor Samuel Tilden. For the occasion, the bartender invented this legendary mixture of bourbon, sweet vermouth and bitters stirred with crushed ice, strained into a martini glass and garnished with a maraschino cherry. A dry Manhattan is made with dry vermouth. A perfect Manhattan, with half dry and half sweet vermouth, is a speciality at Bemelmans Bar in the Carlyle Hotel.

MOJITO

The popular Cuban mojito, which means "little sauce", is an iced cocktail made with fresh mint and sugar that are muddled together, then mixed with lime juice, rum and a splash of soda water.

GIBSON

Long before the martini, there was the Gibson, a very dry martini garnished with a small white onion instead of an olive or a lemon twist, and strained into a martini glass. Charles Connolly, a bartender at New York's Player's Club, allegedly made the drink for the illustrator Charles Dana Gibson around 1900.

BELLINI

CITRON LEMONADE

BIG APPLE MARTINI

BRONX

COSMOPOLITAN

BELLINI

A mixture of white peach nectar and Italian sparkling wine, the Bellini was created by Harry Pickering of Harry's Bar in Venice, Italy, and named for the rosy hues in paintings by Renaissance artist Giovanni Bellini. The aperitif is served at Harry's Bar in New York.

CITRON LEMONADE

This refreshing mix of lemon-infused vodka, fresh lemon juice, sugar syrup, bruised mint, and club soda, served in a tall collins glass, was created by the head bartender at the Lever House in 2004. It has all the makings of a classic.

BIG APPLE MARTINI

Attempts are constantly made to reinvent the martini. Cocktails that dubiously fall into the contemporary category include the watermelon martini, pomegranate martini, and smoky martini (vodka with a splash of smoky, single malt scotch). None have caught on like the Big Apple martini, a mixture of vodka, apple liqueur, and fresh lime juice, garnished with a green apple slice.

BRONX

The little-known Bronx, consisting of gin, orange juice, and both sweet and dry vermouth, was invented at the Waldorf-Astoria as a challenge by a patron. Named for the zoo and not the borough, the drink was popular during its day and is experiencing a mild revival in the hands of bartenders interested in preparing historic cocktails.

COSMOPOLITAN

Although it is not known where or when the cosmopolitan was invented, what is certain is that this pink drink has come to be associated with New York's fashionable set. The cocktail is a mix of vodka (often infused with citrus), Triple Sec, Rose's lime juice, and cranberry juice, served in a martini glass and garnished with a lemon twist. This precursor to the endless variations on the vodka martini served today dates to the late 1980s. The cosmopolitan became all the rage in the 1990s, and its popularity has never waned.

To outside observers, New York's vast restaurant landscape may look like a random, ever-changing terrain. But it is carefully shaped by a handful of trail-blazing restaurateurs and creative chefs who continually strive to create new and exciting culinary experiences that appeal to diners' appetite for invention.

TRENDSETTERS

As the fashion, media, and arts capital of the nation, New York provides fertile ground for influential restaurants and cuisine. This most cosmopolitan of cities is the closest thing there is to a worldwide competitive arena. Young chefs come from all over the world for the chance to climb to the top of their field, while restaurateurs eager to meet, or surpass, New Yorkers' expectations create restaurants in dramatic settings orchestrated by notable designers and architects.

Nearly all of New York's trend-setting restaurants are owned by a select few. Danny Meyer's Union Square Café pioneered the comfort food movement. Diners feel equally welcome in the relaxed atmosphere of his other establishments, which include Gramercy Tavern and Blue Smoke, an upscale restaurant serving authentic Memphis barbecue.

Mario Batali brings a contemporary approach to Italian food at Babbo Ristorante e Enoteca and also presides, along with partner Joseph Bastianich, over restaurants with distinctive menus, from a seafood trattoria to a wine bar (page 59). French-born Daniel Boulud began working in restaurants at the age of fourteen and later studied under such notable French chefs as Roger Vergé. In 1993, after serving as head chef at New York's venerable Le Cirque, he opened Daniel on the Upper East Side, a restaurant that helps define contemporary French cuisine. Daniel was soon followed by the popular and eclectic Café Boulud.

Jean-Georges Vongerichten launched his American career preparing updates of classic French dishes, first at JoJo on the Upper East Side and later at Jean Georges on Central Park West. For his latest themed restaurants,

renowned architects were hired to set the stage. At 66 in Tribeca, reinterpretations of Chinese cuisine are presented against an austere backdrop designed by architect Richard Meier. At Spice Market in the Meatpacking District, Asian street food is served in an expansive, exotic space fashioned by Jacques Garcia. Garcia also created the opulent interior of Vongerichten's V Steakhouse, with its gilded columns, velvet chairs, and crystal chandeliers.

Perhaps New York's most innovative restaurateur, and the one who seems to be cutting the widest path, is Stephen Hanson, head of the B. R. Guest group. His name may not be well known, but his restaurants, including the chic SoHo eatery Fiamma Osteria and Ruby Foo's Dim Sum, are. He now dominates the category of restaurants-as-theatre.

Innovative restaurateurs are masters at creating theatrical dining experiences.

In the Kitchen with Mario Batali

Mario Batali used to write several letters a week apologising to customers of his flagship restaurant, Babbo Ristorante e Enoteca, who complained about the music played during dinner. Customers at Babbo might hear the Grateful Dead, Led Zeppelin and Jane's Addiction while enjoying Batali's acclaimed beef cheek ravioli with crushed pigeon liver and black truffles, and paying hundreds of dollars for a bottle of wine.

Ever one to shirk convention, however, Batali no longer feels he has to justify his taste in music. The qualities that define fine dining, he believes, are changing. "Savvy confidence", he asserts, "will replace haute sweet and sour onions, duck bacon, and *membrillo* vinegar. "It's the duck bacon that does it", he explains, recognising how a well-chosen final ingredient can send diners into ecstasies. He acknowledges that "every course can't be a resounding symphony". Pasta, he believes, is best kept simple. "We live on that bridge between simplicity and excess".

Batali has opinions on everything. About avant-garde, intellectual interpretations of dishes, he says, "Sometimes you've just got to make dinner delicious". Regarding the explosion of theme restaurants, he notes, "A theme isn't a bad thing, as long as it's not

Mario Batali's cooking, despite its European roots, is characterised by a brash confidence that is purely American in spirit. These qualities and his formidable talent in the kitchen have made him a national star and the proprietor of an expanding constellation of restaurants.

cuisine's attention to detail" as the hallmark of fine dining in this country. That can only work to Batali's advantage.

An unrelenting confidence has been a theme in Batali's life. Shortly after graduating from college, he left the United States for Europe. He was apprenticed to Marco Pierre White in London, then studied Italian cooking for three years in a small village in northern Italy. In February of 1992, he returned to the United States, ready to enter the restaurant scene. Becoming one of the most influential chefs of his generation was not Batali's goal, however. He simply knew how to cook and had the courage to do something different.

Batali's approach is to add muliple layers of ingredients until a dish is so far beyond what diners expect that they are transfixed. Sweetbreads, for instance, are served with

a prison term". This determination to follow his convictions has propelled him to the top and brought him numerous awards, including three stars from the *New York Times* and two popular television shows.

Batali's own restaurants, though not theme-based, are intentionally very distinct: an Italian pizzeria in a space that looks like an Italian train station (Otto Enoteca Pizzeria in Greenwich Village); a Roman-style trattoria (Lupa, also in the Village); a southern Italian seafood trattoria (Esca in the Theatre District); a Spanish tapas restaurant (Casa Mono in Gramercy Park); and a wine bar (Bar Jamón, also in Gramercy Park). His newest ventures include an Italian ice cream (gelato) stand and Del Posto in the Meatpacking District, which serves food representing the best of Italian home cooking.

For artisanal cheese makers in the Hudson River Valley and New England, making cheese is not just a living. It is a valued craft, a precise science and a lifestyle choice. New Yorkers embrace these award-winning local cheeses, which are featured at some of the city's finest restaurants.

ARTISANAL CHEESE

Twenty years ago, only a handful of speciality shops, such as Ideal Cheese Shop and Murray's Cheese Shop, exclusively sold cheese, most of it imported. With the growing interest in artisanal foods of all kinds, a small number of individuals, having sampled the finest cheeses of Europe, dedicated themselves to learning the craft of making small batches of cheese by hand according to time-honoured recipes and techniques. They started dairy farms in upstate New York and New England, where they could earn a livelihood by making high-quality products. Today, over a hundred artisanal cheese makers are located in New York and throughout New England.

Cheese made from the milk of grass-fed animals has an herbaceous quality that changes subtly with the seasons and the pastures where the animals graze. The northeastern United States, with its rich, alluvial soil, sweet spring water and diverse vegetation, provides pasturage ideal for grazing herds of sheep, goats, and cows. Taking advantage of these resources, Vermont Shepherd became the first local cheese-maker to gain national attention, in the early 1990s, with its Pyrenees-style raw sheep's milk cheese. New England – Vermont in particular – is now regarded as the most important cheese-making region in the nation.

As artisanal producers gained recognition for their cheeses, restaurants started to bring the new offerings to the attention of diners. In 1993, Terrance Brennan opened Picholine near Lincoln Center, a restaurant with its own cheese cellar. Brennan is widely credited as being the first restaurateur to take the cheese course seriously. At Picholine, diners are presented at the conclusion of their meals with a detailed cheese menu. In 2001, Brennan opened the Artisanal Fromagerie and Bistro, a restaurant and shop where more than three hundred domestic and imported cheeses are stored and aged in five cheese cellars. Today, many of the city's fine restaurants offer a sophisticated selection of cheeses after dinner. Colin Alevras of The Tasting Room and Dan Barber of Blue Hill in Greenwich Village, for instance, pride themselves on sourcing local artisanal cheeses.

Long-standing Italian cheese shops such as Joe's Dairy in SoHo and Alleva Dairy and DiPalo's Fine Foods in Little Italy carry on the tradition of making fresh mozzarella and ricotta daily, as they have for more than a century. These shops have large retail followings and provide many restaurants with fresh cheese.

RONNYBROOK FARM
DAIRY YOGURT

SPROUT CREEK DAIRY BARAT

SPROUT CREEK DAIRY OURAY

UP A CREEK FARM ABBEY RAW
SHEEP'S MILK CHEESE

OLD CHATHAM SHEEPHERDING COMPANY
SHEEP'S MILK RICOTTA

COACH FARM GOAT CHEESE

RONNYBROOK FARM
DAIRY YOGHURT

The diet of the cows at this family-run farm in the Hudson River Valley enhances the flavour of the dairy's tangy yoghurt, whether whole milk or non-fat. Ronnybrook also makes drinkable fruit-flavoured yoghurt.

OLD CHATHAM SHEEPHERDING
COMPANY SHEEP'S MILK RICOTTA

Old Chatham, in the Hudson River Valley, makes what may be the creamiest sheep's milk ricotta outside Italy. Most of the production goes to chefs, who appreciate the tangy bite and complex flavour.

SPROUT CREEK DAIRY OURAY

Located in the Hudson River Valley, Sprout Creek Dairy is both a working farm and an educational facility. Wheels of ouray, aged three to five months, have a small surface-to-volume ratio, giving the dense cheese a creamy, buttery flavour.

SPROUT CREEK DAIRY BARAT

Weighing 185 to 250 grams each (6–8 oz), the small wheels of barat develop a complex, nutty flavour with the sharpness of farmhouse Cheddar after only three to four months of aging. The cheese has a dry, firm, crumbly texture.

COACH FARM GOAT'S CHEESE

Since the mid-1980s, Coach Farm, in the Hudson River Valley, has been making fresh goat's cheese. Over time, the family farm has grown to include a herd of more than a thousand French Alpine goats, a breed that produces milk with high butterfat and protein content, ideal for cheese-making. Coach Farm products now include aged goat's cheese and goat's cheese chunks marinated in olive oil and herbs. The triple cream, at 75 percent butterfat, has a buttery texture and flavour. Coach Farm cheeses features by name on the menus of many of New York's best restaurants.

UP A CREEK FARM ABBEY RAW
SHEEP'S MILK CHEESE

This raw sheep's milk cheese, aged four to six months, is the sole product of Vermont cheese-makers Frankie and Mary Beth Whitten. It has a nutty flavour and smooth texture reminiscent of Gruyère, with grassy undertones and a pleasantly light sharpness to the finish. The cheese is best served on a cheese plate accompanied by something sweet, such as quince paste. The recipe was given by a monastery to the Belgian cheese-maker who taught the Whittens how to make the cheese.

SPROUT CREEK DAIRY TOUSSAINT

JOE'S DAIRY SMOKED MOZZARELLA

JOE'S DAIRY FRESH MOZZARELLA

VERMONT BUTTER AND CHEESE COMPANY CULTURED BUTTER

Vermont Butter & Cheese COMPANY Cultured Butter UNSALTED

HAWTHORNE VALLEY QUARK

BERKSHIRE BLUE

VERMONT BUTTER AND CHEESE COMPANY MASCARPONE

SPROUT CREEK DAIRY TOUSSAINT

The recipe for this cheese is identical to that for ouray. Toussaint is aged for three to five months, but the large, flat shape of the wheel gives the cheese a distinctly sharp, complex flavour when ripened.

BERKSHIRE BLUE

Michael G. Miller produces this cheese at the Berkshire Cheese Company in Lenox, Massachusetts. The raw, Jersey cow's milk cheese is modelled after Exmoor blue, traditionally made in Taunton, Somerset. Aged nine weeks, a short time for a blue, it is smoother in flavour and is less salty than other blue cheeses.

JOE'S DAIRY FRESH MOZZARELLA

The fresh rounds of creamy mozzarella made daily at Joe's Dairy in SoHo are among the best produced in the city. The dairy uses whole cow's milk, and each stage of the process is performed by hand to ensure quality and consistency.

JOE'S DAIRY SMOKED MOZZARELLA

Five days a week, the smoky scent of hickory wafts from Joe's Dairy as owner Anthony Campanelli oversees the production of smoked mozzarella. The smoked cheese retains the creaminess of the fresh cheese but is intensely flavoured by the hickory.

HAWTHORNE VALLEY QUARK

Hawthorne Valley Farm in upstate New York is part of the larger Hawthorne Valley Association, known primarily for its commitment to raising animals free of hormones and antibiotics and for its organic farmhouse products. Quark, which comes from the German word for "curd", is a soft fresh cheese in the same family as fromage blanc and crème fraîche. One of the farm's specialities, quark has the texture of sour cream and a flavour somewhere between sour cream and yoghurt. It can be used in place of crème fraîche or ricotta cheese.

VERMONT BUTTER AND CHEESE COMPANY MASCARPONE

A pioneer in the artisanal cheese movement, the Vermont Butter and Cheese Company produces a wide range of products. One is mascarpone, a triple cream Italian cheese made from cream and possessing a mild, slightly sweet flavour.

VERMONT BUTTER AND CHEESE COMPANY CULTURED BUTTER

This lightly salted butter, churned in small batches from Vermont cream, is similar to French butter in its high butterfat content of 86 percent, its low water content and its rich flavour and aroma.

CPR KIT
AVAILABLE
BEHIND BAR

LIQUOR BAR

CHOKING VICTIM

APPETISERS AND SMALL PLATES

New Yorkers have an abiding fondness for updated classics. Yet they

cannot resist a new appetiser or hors d'oeuvre made by an innovative chef.

Whether served in restaurants or prepared at home, appetisers and hors d'oeuvres tend to be traditional, with contemporary versions of classics such as spanikopita, buffalo (chicken) wings and clams (cockles) casino being a prevailing theme. Chefs also like to create pairings of seasonal ingredients – polenta with chanterelles, foie gras with caramelised onions and sea scallops with radicchio. Dishes such as prawns with slaw, tomato tart made with puff pastry and spicy sesame noodles are so satisfying that diners might order an appetiser and an hors d'oeuvre in place of a main course.

HEIRLOOM TOMATO TARTS WITH GOAT CHEESE

Heirloom tomatoes, which go by intriguing names such as Banana Legs, Extra Eros Zlatolaska, and Radiator Charlie's Mortgage Lifter, come in myriad shapes and a rainbow of colours. They are grown for their incomparable flavour, not for how well they travel to market or how long a shelf life they might have. During the tomato season – July to September – New York's finest restaurants, including Gramercy Tavern, Aureole, and The Grocery showcase the varieties grown at local Blooming Hills Farm or Eckerton Hills Farms.

1 Preheat the oven to 200°C (400°F). In a small bowl, combine two-thirds of the basil strips, the chopped garlic and the halved small tomatoes. Add the olive oil, season to taste with salt and toss gently. Set aside. Reserve the remaining basil strips.

2 Place the puff dough on a lightly floured work surface. Cut the sheet into 6 rectangles, each about 10 x 13 cm (4 x 5 inches). Place the rectangles on a baking sheet and prick them all over with a fork to prevent the dough from rising. Bake until light golden brown, 10–12 minutes. Remove from the oven and let stand on the baking sheet. Leave the oven on.

3 Meanwhile, in a small bowl, use a fork to mash the goat's cheese. Slowly pour in the milk, stirring until the cheese mixture has a smooth consistency, but is not runny. You may not need all of the milk.

4 Cut the large tomatoes into slices 12 mm (½ inch) thick and season with salt. Spoon 1 heaped tablespoon of the goat's cheese mixture on to each pastry rectangle and gently spread to cover the surface. Using only the large, centre tomato slices (reserve the remainder for another use), place a slice on each tart. Bake the tarts until warmed through, about 5 minutes.

5 Place the tarts on individual plates. Season the tomato quarters with salt and scatter them around the tarts, dividing evenly. Top each tart with a mound of the tomato-and-basil mixture, again dividing evenly. Drizzle olive oil over the tomatoes. Scatter the reserved basil strips around each plate and serve at once.

Serve with a spicy, medium-bodied Cabernet Franc.

20–25 fresh basil leaves, cut into thin strips

2 cloves garlic, finely chopped

375 g (12 oz) mixed small heirloom or cherry tomatoes, halved

60 ml (2 fl oz) extra-virgin olive oil, plus more for drizzling

Sea salt

1 sheet good-quality frozen puff dough, about 25 x 30 cm (10 x 12 inches), partially thawed

155 g (5 oz) fresh goat's cheese

About 125 ml (4 fl oz) whole milk

1 large red heirloom tomato such as black krim, brandywine, or purple Cherokee

1 large yellow or white heirloom tomato such as Hugh's or great white

6 green zebra tomatoes or other medium tomatoes, quartered

Makes 6 servings

Urban Gardening

Accustomed to making creative use of small spaces, New Yorkers plant potted herbs on rooftops and fire escapes, corn in window boxes, and tomatoes in tiny backyards. Even abandoned vacant lots seem to sprout spontaneously with urban gardens. Establishing them is not just a hobby; it is also a political act. The Green Thumb, Green Guerillas, and Just Food's City Farms take over empty lots, primarily in economically disadvantaged areas, and turn them into sources of fresh food. The harvest is given to the community members that tend the gardens. Hundreds of such gardens can be found throughout the five boroughs.

The most famous use of a small, urban space for agricultural purposes is Eli Zabar's rooftop garden. Zabar is the founder and owner of the deli E.A.T., Eli's Bread, and the Vinegar Factory (his father founded the eponymously named store on the Upper West Side). In the early 1990s, longing for sun-warmed, ripe tomatoes, he decided to plant a few vines on the roof of the Vinegar Factory. Pleased with the tomatoes, he expanded his urban farm. It now includes a bounty of beans, beetroot, and other produce.

SPINACH AND FETA ROLLS

Greek-run diners and coffee shops are part of the fabric of New York. They serve familiar food such as pancakes and omelettes, along with American cakes and pies displayed in rotating glass cases. The kitchens also turn out delicious home-style Greek fare, including gyros (döner kebab) wrapped in pitta bread, crunchy salads piled high on the plate and dressed with a tangy vinaigrette, the aubergine casserole known as moussaka and, always, spanikopita, the spinach-and-feta-cheese pie made with phyllo. When made for individual servings, it is the ideal appetiser or first course.

2 kg (4 lb) spinach (about 4 bunches)

Sea salt and freshly ground pepper

60 ml (2 fl oz) extra-virgin olive oil

1 large yellow onion, finely chopped

30 g (1 oz) finely chopped fresh flat-leaf parsley

10 g (⅓ oz) finely chopped fresh dill

3 spring onions, white and pale green parts only, finely chopped

75 g (2½ oz) pine nuts

250 g (8 oz) feta cheese, crumbled

6 sheets phyllo dough, each about 30 x 45 cm (12 x 18 inches), thawed overnight in the refrigerator if frozen

60 g (2 oz) unsalted butter, melted

Makes 6 servings

1 Rinse the spinach in 2 or 3 changes of water, discarding the tough stems and any damaged leaves. Drain briefly in a colander. Bring a large pot of water to the boil over high heat. Generously salt the water. Add the spinach and stir until all the spinach has wilted, about 1 minute. Transfer the spinach to a colander and rinse under cold water. Using your hands, squeeze out the excess moisture. Transfer to a cutting board and roughly chop. Place in a large bowl.

2 In a frying pan over medium-high heat, heat the olive oil. Add the yellow onion and cook until transparent and lightly browned, 6–8 minutes. Stir in the parsley, dill, and spring onions and season to taste with salt and pepper. Transfer to the bowl and toss with the spinach to combine.

3 Place the pine nuts in a dry frying pan over medium heat and toast, shaking the pan occasionally, until fragrant and golden, 5–7 minutes. Add the pine nuts to the spinach. Add the feta and toss to combine.

4 Preheat the oven to 190°C (375°F). Have ready a rimmed baking sheet or Swiss roll tin lined with non-stick baking paper. Cut the phyllo sheets in half lengthways, then stack them between sheets of non-stick baking paper and cover with a lightly dampened kitchen towel to prevent them from becoming brittle. Working with half a sheet at a time, brush lightly with melted butter. Add a tablespoon of the spinach filling to one end of the phyllo sheet, leaving a 12-mm (½-inch) border at the edges. Fold the sides of the phyllo over the filling, then roll into a cylinder. Place on the baking sheet seam side down. Use a sharp knife to cut 2 diagonal slits in the top of each roll. Lightly brush the tops with the rest of the melted butter.

5 Bake until golden, 20–25 minutes. Let cool on the pan for 5–10 minutes. Serve warm on individual plates or a serving platter.

Serve with a spicy red wine such as Cabernet Franc.

SAUTÉED FOIE GRAS WITH CARAMELIZED ONIONS AND GRAPES

The Hudson River Valley, north of New York City, contains a bounty of culinary resources, from apple-farmers to wine-makers to small-scale food producers. Waldy Malouf, author of The Hudson River Valley Cookbook, *cooked in many of Manhattan's best kitchens, including The Four Seasons, La Côte Basque, and the St. Regis Hotel, before opening Beacon Restaurant in Midtown, where he specialises in foods of the Hudson River Valley. Foie gras produced by Hudson Valley Foie Gras, known across the nation as one of the best, is a staple menu item at the Beacon, which serves a version of this recipe using local apples.*

1 Carefully peel any remaining patches of membrane from the foie gras. If there are two lobes of foie gras, gently pull them apart. If they do not separate easily, use a knife to sever the veins that hold them together. Examine the areas inside the folds; if you see any green bile, remove it with a knife. (This is very important, as even a speck of bile can make the entire liver taste bitter.) Gently feel inside each lobe with your fingertips. When you locate the large vein, carefully pull it out, following it along with your fingertips. The vein may have a few branches that go in various directions; remove as many of them as you can.

2 Using a large, sharp knife, cut the foie gras cross-ways into 12 slices, each about 12 mm (½ inch) thick. Wrap the slices in clingfilm and refrigerate until ready to use.

3 Bring a saucepan three-quarters full of water to the boil. Add the onions, return the water to the boil and cook for 1 minute. Using a slotted spoon, transfer the onions to a colander, rinse under cold water and drain. Using a sharp knife, trim the root and stem ends of each onion. Pinch each onion to slip it from the skin. Return the water to the boil, salt the water, add the peeled onions and cook until tender, about 8 minutes. Drain, rinse under cold running water and drain again. Set aside.

4 In a sauté pan, melt the butter over medium heat. Add the onions and honey and sauté, constantly tossing and swirling the onions in the pan, until golden brown and caramelised, about 5 minutes. Set aside.

5 Heat another sauté pan over high heat until very hot. Season both sides of the foie gras slices with salt and pepper. Place the slices in the hot pan and sear until caramelised and brown, 1–2 minutes. Turn and sear on the second side until caramelised and brown, 1–2 minutes. Transfer to a plate and cover loosely with aluminium foil to keep warm.

6 Add the reserved onions, grapes, stock, vinegar, and brandy to the sauté pan, bring to the boil over medium-high heat, and cook until the liquid thickens, about 5 minutes.

7 Arrange one or two slices of toast on individual plates. Set a slice of foie gras on top of each toast. Arrange the onions and grapes around the foie gras. Spoon the sauce over the foie gras. Serve at once.

Serve with a late-harvest white such as Riesling or Gewürztraminer.

450 g (1 lb) fresh goose or duck foie gras

375 g (12 oz) pearl onions

Sea salt and freshly ground pepper

2 tablespoons unsalted butter

2 tablespoons honey

4 small bunches seedless white or red grapes

250 ml (8 fl oz) chicken stock

60 ml (2 fl oz) white wine vinegar

2 tablespoons brandy

12 slices French-style bread, each about 12 mm (½ inch) thick, toasted

Makes 6–12 servings

CLAMS CASINO

Clams Casino, an East Coast tradition, is said to have originated in the early 1900s at the Narragansett Pier Casino. Perhaps because of the availability of local clams — at the time, New York was the nation's leading clam producer, with the majority harvested in the waters near Manhattan and Long Island — it became a standard antipasto offering throughout New York. Today, the dish is still a staple on dinner menus in Little Italy and on Arthur Avenue, an Italian-American neighbourhood in the Bronx. Clams Casino is usually made with small littleneck clams, named after Littleneck Bay on Long Island.

1 small red sweet pepper

28–30 littleneck or
18–24 cherrystone clams
or cockles well scrubbed

250 ml (8 fl oz) dry white wine

3 sprigs fresh flat-leaf parsley

1.5–2 kg (3–4 lb) coarse or
rock salt

FOR THE TOPPING

4 rashers streaky bacon

1 tablespoon unsalted butter

2 tablespoons olive oil

1 small yellow onion, finely
chopped

2 cloves garlic, finely chopped

½ teaspoon dried oregano,
crumbled

2 teaspoons red wine vinegar

2 tablespoons freshly grated
Parmesan cheese

1 tablespoon finely chopped fresh
flat-leaf parsley

Sea salt and freshly ground pepper

Makes 6 servings

1 Preheat the grill. Place the red sweet pepper on a baking sheet lined with aluminium foil and slip it under the grill about 15 cm (6 inches) from the heat source. Grill, turning as needed, until blackened on all sides. Set aside until cool enough to handle, then peel, removing nearly all traces of charred skin. Do not rinse the pepper. Halve and remove the stem, seeds and ribs, then dice the pepper and set it aside.

2 Discard any clams that do not close to the touch. Put the clams in a large saucepan along with the wine and parsley sprigs. Bring to the boil over high heat, then reduce the heat to medium, cover and steam, shaking the pan occasionally, until the clams open, 4–5 minutes. Remove from the heat and discard any clams that have failed to open. Set aside to cool.

3 Cover the bottom of a rimmed baking sheet or large baking tin with a 12-mm (½-inch) layer of coarse salt. When the clams are cool enough to touch, remove and discard the top shell, leaving the clam meat in the bottom shell. Place the clams in their shells on the salt, pushing them into the salt so they are stable.

4 To make the topping, in a heavy frying pan over medium-low heat, fry the bacon rashers, turning occasionally, until crisp, 7–8 minutes. Transfer to absorbent paper to drain. In a large sauté pan over medium heat, melt the butter with the olive oil.

Add the onion and sauté until tender and translucent, 5–7 minutes. Add the garlic and oregano and sauté just until the garlic is light golden and fragrant, about 2 minutes. Crumble in the bacon and stir in the diced pepper, vinegar, Parmesan, chopped parsley, and salt and pepper to taste. Remove from the heat.

5 Preheat the grill again. Spoon the topping over the clams, dividing it evenly. Place under the grill about 15 cm (6 inches) from the heat source. Grill until the topping is heated through, about 4 minutes.

6 To serve, cover a large platter with a 12-mm (½-inch) layer of coarse or rock salt. Using tongs, place the hot clams on the salt, pushing them into the salt so they are stable. Serve at once.

Serve with a dry, fruity white wine such as Sauvignon Blanc.

SPICY SESAME NOODLES

Ordering Chinese food delivered to your door is a ritual in New York, and no order is complete without a container of these noodles covered in a sweet, silken sauce peppered with chillies. Although the origin of this iconic dish is unknown, Hunan and Sichuan versions are found at many Chinese restaurants. Chef Jean-Georges Vongerichten serves his own version – thin vermicelli topped with peanut sauce, cucumber, green apple and spring onions – at his pan-Chinese restaurant called 66 in Tribeca.

1 Bring a large pot of water to the boil over high heat. Generously salt the water, add the fresh noodles and a few drops of sesame oil. Stir the noodles to prevent them from sticking, and cook until tender, about 3 minutes. (If using dried pasta, follow the timing on the packet instructions.) Drain and rinse thoroughly under cold running water, then drain again. Transfer the noodles to a large bowl, add 2 tablespoons of the sesame oil and toss to coat. Cover and refrigerate until chilled, at least 1 hour.

2 In a food processor or blender, combine the remaining 2 tablespoons of sesame oil, 1 teaspoon sea salt, peanut butter, tahini, rice vinegar, chilli oil, jalapeño, ginger, garlic, sugar, pepper and the brewed tea or chicken stock and process until smooth. Add more tea or stock, if necessary, to make a sauce that is liquid enough to coat the noodles. Season to taste with additional salt and pepper if needed.

3 Peel and seed the cucumber and cut into 5-cm (2-inch) matchstick strips. Peel the carrots and cut into 5-cm (2-inch) matchsticks.

4 Just before serving, add the sauce, cucumbers, carrots and spring onions to the noodles and toss to coat evenly. If the noodles are sticky, add more tea or stock and toss again. Serve at once, garnished with coriander, if desired.

Serve with a dry white wine such as Gewürztraminer or a light-bodied microbrew beer.

Sea salt

450 g (1 lb) fresh or dried Chinese egg noodles or dried linguine

4 tablespoons Asian sesame oil, plus more for cooking

235 g (7½ oz) smooth peanut butter

2 teaspoons tahini

2 tablespoons rice vinegar

1 tablespoon Asian chilli oil or Hunan pepper sauce

1 jalapeño chilli, halved and seeded

2–3 tablespoons peeled and grated fresh ginger

1 garlic clove, peeled and chopped

2 tablespoons sugar

1 teaspoon freshly ground white or black pepper

250 ml (8 fl oz) brewed black tea or chicken stock, or as needed, at room temperature

1 long cucumber

3 small carrots

2 spring onions, white and pale green parts only, thinly sliced

Fresh coriander leaves for garnish (optional)

Makes 6 servings

Ordering Out

If there is one thing that distinguishes eating at home in New York from eating at home anywhere else in the country, and maybe the world, it's that New Yorkers can get whatever food they crave delivered to their door or their desk. Dining in often begins not with turning on the stove, but with flipping through the take-away menus surreptitiously slipped under their doors. Thai curries, Japanese sushi, Greek mezedes, Italian pastas, Indian vindaloos, Mexican moles, and southern barbecue – the selection is vast. Despite this, Chinese food, chiefly Hunan, Sichuan and Cantonese, is still the mainstay of New York take-away.

Ordering food is such a ritual of office culture that many large companies have a policy of picking up the bill for dinner delivered to employees working late at their desks. Neighbourhood eateries are as willing as restaurants to deliver food, rarely with a minimum charge. If a customer orders it, they will bring it, whether a pint of ice cream or a turkey sandwich. Delivery people peddling their bicycles around the city, a bag hanging from each handlebar, are as much a part of the street scene as yellow taxis.

BAY SCALLOPS WITH PANCETTA, RADICCHIO, AND PESTO

Jonathan Waxman, who impressed New Yorkers in the 1980s at Jams on the Upper West Side, is back with Barbuto, his restaurant in the West Village. He previously lived in Northern California, and his cooking is rooted in the practise of taking the best local, seasonal ingredients and combining them in sublime ways. During the summer months, Waxman serves local bay scallops, harvested in the waters surrounding Long Island. He sears the delicate shellfish quickly to retain their sweet, nutty flavour and serves them with juicy tomatoes, crunchy radicchio and a simplified basil pesto.

FOR THE PESTO

60 g (2 oz) fresh basil leaves

2 cloves garlic

125 ml (14 fl oz) extra-virgin olive oil

1 kg (2 lb) scallops, off the shell

2 tablespoons unsalted butter

115 g (¼ lb) pancetta, cut into strips 6 mm (¼ inch) wide

1–2 heads radicchio, cored and cut into thin strips

2 large tomatoes, peeled and seeded (page 187), then finely diced

Makes 6–8 servings

1 To make the pesto, put the basil and garlic in a blender or food processor and process to chop very finely. Add the olive oil and process to make a paste that still has some texture. Scrape the pesto into a bowl and set aside.

2 Rinse the scallops and pat dry. In a large sauté pan over medium heat, melt the butter and heat until golden. Add the pancetta and sauté until golden brown, 2–3 minutes. Transfer to a small plate. Increase the heat to medium-high, add the scallops and cook, turning once, until golden, about 2 minutes per side. Add the pesto and pancetta and toss quickly to coat the scallops. Add the radicchio and mix well.

3 Divide the scallops and radicchio among warmed individual plates, top with the tomatoes and serve at once.

Serve with a crisp rosé such as Wolffer Estates or Channing Daughters.

GRAVLAX WITH MUSTARD-DILL SAUCE

New Yorkers have a love affair with salmon, whether the classic lox (smoked salmon) on bagels; the grilled, seared or poached fillets common on many menus; or the salmon tartare served at Asian-inspired restaurants. Gravlax, salmon cured in salt, sugar, and dill, is a Swedish dish traditionally accompanied by a mustard-dill sauce as an appetiser. Marcus Samuelsson, of Aquavit in Midtown, is the Swedish culinary ambassador to New York. This recipe, based on one of his favourites, adds coriander and fennel seeds as well as fresh fennel to the seasonings. Serve the gravlax with crispbread, if desired.

1 Using a mortar and pestle, lightly crush the peppercorns, coriander and fennel seeds. Stir in the sugar and salt. Run your fingers gently over the salmon fillet to locate the pin bones and remove them with sturdy tweezers or needle-nosed pliers. Place the salmon in a shallow dish, rub a handful of the salt mixture into both sides, and arrange the fillet skin side down. Sprinkle with the remaining salt mixture.

2 Cut off the stems and feathery leaves from the fennel bulb and discard. Discard the outer layer of the bulb if it is tough, and cut away any discoloured parts. Quarter the bulb lengthways and cut away any tough base portions. Cut the quarters lengthways into slices 6 mm (¼ inch) wide. Coarsely chop the bunches of dill and the coriander sprigs. Cover the salmon with the fennel slices, dill, and coriander. Cover the dish and let stand in a cool, dark place for 6 hours. Transfer to the refrigerator and let cure for at least 30 hours or up to 36 hours.

3 To make the mustard-dill sauce, in a blender or food processor, combine the mustards, sugar, vinegar, coffee, a pinch of salt, and a pinch of pepper. With the machine running, add the oil in a slow, steady stream and process until the sauce is thick and creamy. Transfer to a bowl and stir in the dill. Cover and refrigerate for at least 4 hours or up to overnight to allow the flavours to marry.

4 To serve, scrape the seasonings off the gravlax. Cut it against the grain into thin slices. Serve chilled on individual plates with the mustard sauce on the side. Garnish with lemon wedges and a sprig of dill, if desired.

Serve with a glass of chilled aquavit or a very dry, full-bodied sparkling wine.

2 tablespoons white peppercorns

1 tablespoon coriander seeds

1 tablespoon fennel seeds

250 g (8 oz) sugar

125 g (4 oz) sea salt

1 salmon fillet, 1.25–1.5 kg (2½–3 lb), skin on

1 fennel bulb

2 bunches fresh dill with stems

4 sprigs fresh coriander

FOR THE MUSTARD-DILL SAUCE

2 tablespoons honey mustard

2 teaspoons Dijon mustard

1 tablespoon sugar

1½ tablespoons white wine vinegar

1 tablespoon brewed espresso or strong coffee, chilled

Sea salt and freshly ground pepper

180 ml (6 fl oz) grapeseed or rapeseed oil

15 g (½ oz) chopped fresh dill

Lemon wedges and fresh dill sprigs for garnish (optional)

Makes 10–12 servings

SHRIMP WITH CITRUS AIOLI AND RADICCHIO AND ENDIVE SLAW

Mary Redding, owner and chef of Mary's Fish Camp, is a native Floridian whose cheery little restaurant, located on a picturesque corner in the West Village, caters to New Yorkers with a penchant for seafood. Customers line up before the place opens, waiting to enjoy such coastal fare as oysters on the half-shell, cod sandwiches, lobster rolls and lobster pot pies. Mary uses seasonal, local varieties from up and down the eastern seaboard, including Florida stone crabs and lobster from Long Island to Maine. These crisp prawns – served with citrus aïoli and crunchy cole slaw – are a house favourite.

FOR THE AÏOLI

1 large egg yolk

250 ml (8 fl oz) rapeseed oil

1 tablespoon *each* grated lemon zest and lime zest

2 tablespoons *each* fresh lemon juice and lime juice

Sea salt and freshly ground pepper

FOR THE COLE SLAW

2 heads chicory (witloof)

1 head radicchio, shredded

20 g (¾ oz) chopped fresh flat-leaf parsley

1 tablespoon *each* chopped fresh oregano, thyme, and tarragon

3 tablespoons extra-virgin olive oil

1 tablespoon sherry vinegar

1 teaspoon Dijon mustard

12 prawns or scampi

Peanut oil and rapeseed oil for deep-frying

155 g (5 oz) plain flour

60 g (2 oz) matzo meal or crispbread crumbs

Makes 4 servings

1 To make the aïoli, in a bowl, whisk the egg yolk until smooth. Whisking constantly, begin adding the oil drop by drop. Once an emulsion has formed, add the remaining oil in a thin, steady stream while continuing to whisk. Add the lemon and lime zests and juices and whisk until incorporated. Season to taste with salt and pepper. Cover and refrigerate until ready to use.

2 To make the cole slaw, halve the chicory heads, cut out the cores, then slice the leaves crossways into strips 6-mm (¼-inch) wide. In a bowl, combine the chicory, radicchio, parsley, oregano, thyme, and tarragon. In a small bowl, whisk together the olive oil, sherry vinegar, and mustard. Season to taste with salt and pepper. Drizzle this over the chicory and radicchio and toss to coat. Cover and refrigerate while you prepare the prawns.

3 Working with 1 prawn at a time and using a pair of sharp kitchen scissors, cut along the back of the shell. Gently loosen the shell from both sides, but leave the shell and tail in place. Lift out and discard the dark, vein-like intestinal tract. Rinse the prawns under cold water. Pat dry with kitchen towels.

4 In a large, heavy frying pan over high heat, pour in equal amounts of peanut oil and rapeseed oil to reach a depth of 4 cm (1½ inches). Heat to 180°C (350°F) on a deep-frying thermometer.

5 In a bowl, mix together the flour and matzo meal or crispbread crumbs. Add the prawns and toss to coat. Remove each prawn, shaking off the excess flour mixture. Place in the hot oil and fry, turning once, until the shells are light gold and the prawns are pink, about 3 minutes. Using a slotted spoon, transfer to kitchen towels to drain for about 10 seconds. While the prawns are still hot, generously season both sides with salt and pepper.

6 Divide the cole slaw among individual plates. Place 3 prawns and a dollop of aïoli on each plate. Serve at once.

Serve with a crisp, citrusy white wine such as Seyval Blanc.

BUFFALO WINGS

In 1964, the owner of the Anchor Bar in Buffalo, New York, was intent on preparing a bar snack for her son and his friends. She took wings, a cut of chicken usually relegated to the stockpot, deep-fried them then tossed them in a spicy "secret sauce". Today, wings are standard New York City bar fare at places like Fanelli's, a SoHo institution, and Chumley's, the former speakeasy in the West Village. This classic version, served with celery and blue cheese dip, is updated with harissa and fennel, as well as sweet pepper and carrot sticks.

1 Cut off the stems and leaves from the fennel bulb and discard. Discard the outer layer of the bulb if it is tough and cut away any discoloured areas. Quarter the bulb lengthways and cut away any tough base portions. Cut the quarters lengthways into thin strips. Immerse the fennel, celery, carrots, and sweet pepper in a bowl of ice water to chill for at least 30 minutes.

2 To make the blue cheese dip, in a small bowl, whisk together the mayonnaise and buttermilk. Stir in the blue cheese and season to taste with salt and pepper. Cover and refrigerate until serving.

3 Cut off the tip of each chicken wing; discard or reserve for stock. Cut the wing in half at the joint to make 2 pieces. Rinse and pat dry with kitchen towels.

4 In a heavy saucepan over medium heat, melt the butter with the hot-pepper sauce. Stir in the vinegar, harissa (if using), Tabasco sauce, and ¼ teaspoon pepper. Remove from the heat and set aside.

5 In a large, heavy frying pan over high heat, pour in enough oil to reach a depth of 2.5 cm (1 inch). Heat to 190°C (375ºF) on a deep-frying thermometer. Working in batches to avoid crowding, carefully add a single layer of chicken pieces and fry, turning the pieces often with tongs, until golden brown and crisp, 6–8 minutes. Transfer to kitchen towels to drain.

6 Toss the chicken pieces in the butter mixture. Transfer to a serving platter. Drain the vegetables and arrange on the platter. Serve with the dip.

Serve with a full-bodied beer such as Brooklyn Lager.

1 fennel bulb

4 celery stalks, halved and cut into 10-cm (4-inch) sticks

4 carrots, peeled, halved and cut into 10-cm (4-inch) sticks

1 red sweet pepper, seeded and cut into thin strips

FOR THE BLUE CHEESE DIP

125 ml (4 fl oz) mayonnaise

125 ml (4 fl oz) buttermilk

125 ml (4 oz) blue cheese, crumbled

Sea salt and freshly ground pepper

1.5 kg (3 lb) chicken wings

60 g (2 oz) unsalted butter

60 ml (2 fl oz) hot-pepper sauce

1 tablespoon apple cider vinegar

1 teaspoon harissa (optional)

Dash of Tabasco sauce

Freshly ground pepper

Rapeseed oil for deep-frying

Makes 6 servings

New York's Microbreweries

Just over a century ago, New York City had seventy-seven breweries, nearly fifty of them located in Brooklyn. At the time of Prohibition, they were so numerous in the borough's Williamsburg neighbourhood that a ten-square-block was dubbed "Brewers' Row". Over the following decades, however, the city's beer-brewing industry slowly dwindled. But in 1996, brewing returned with the opening of the Brooklyn Brewery in a former steel foundry in Williamsburg. The name Brewers' Row, also revived, now refers to North Eleventh Street, where the brewery is situated. Brooklyn Lager is Brooklyn Brewery's best-known product, but like many microbreweries, it makes special seasonal beers, including Pumpkin Ale, a colonial brew with the colour and aroma of pumpkin.

From the Carnegie Hill Brewing Company uptown to the Chelsea Brewing Company downtown, brewpubs can be found throughout the city. Bierkraft, in Brooklyn, is a pub that specialises in microbrews. Among the hundreds of offerings are beers from Blue Point Brewing in Patchogue and Southampton Publick House, both on Long Island.

POLENTA CROSTINI WITH CHANTERELLES

Polenta in many forms – soft and creamy or turned into crispy cakes, enriched with mascarpone or pecorino cheese – appears on the menus of many restaurants, whether their speciality is Italian, French or American cuisine. The subtle flavour of polenta makes it the perfect bed for sautéed vegetables, grilled meat or mushrooms such as the chanterelles that top these bite-sized polenta crostini. The golden mushrooms have the aroma of apricots and are said to taste more like a flower than a mushroom. Foraged in upstate New York, they begin showing up on menus in the summer and last until late autumn.

FOR THE POLENTA

1 bay leaf

Sea salt and freshly ground pepper

2 tablespoons olive oil

155 g (5 oz) polenta

1 tablespoon unsalted butter

FOR THE MUSHROOMS

60 g (2 oz) unsalted butter

3 shallots, minced

250 g (½ lb) chanterelle mushrooms, brushed clean, trimmed, and roughly chopped

Sea salt and freshly ground pepper

125 g (¼ lb) mascarpone cheese

2 tablespoons finely chopped fresh flat-leaf parsley

Wedge of Parmesan cheese

Makes 8–10 servings

1 To make the polenta, in a saucepan, bring 1 l (32 fl oz) water to the boil over medium-high heat. Add the bay leaf, 1 tablespoon salt, and 1 tablespoon of the olive oil. Gradually add the polenta in a thin, steady stream, whisking constantly to prevent lumps. When all the polenta has been added, reduce the heat to low and continue stirring with a wooden spoon until it is as thick as porridge and pulls away from the sides of the pan, about 30 minutes. Discard the bay leaf.

2 Rinse a 20-by-25-cm (8-x-10-inch) ceramic or glass baking dish but do not dry it. Immediately pour the polenta into the dish. It should be about 12 mm (½ inch) thick. Set aside to cool until firm, about 30 minutes.

3 Just before serving, prepare the mushrooms: In a large sauté pan over medium heat, melt the 4 tablespoons butter. Add the shallots and sauté until slightly wilted, about 2 minutes. Add the chanterelles, season with salt and pepper and sauté until golden brown and tender, about 4 minutes. Remove from the heat and set aside.

4 Cut the cooled polenta into slices about 2.5 cm x 5 cm (1 inch x 2 inches). In a large frying pan over medium-high heat, melt the butter with the remaining olive oil. Working in batches, fry the slices until barely golden, about 3 minutes per side.

5 Arrange the polenta on a platter. Place a dollop of mascarpone on each piece. Spoon the mushrooms over the mascarpone, dividing them evenly, and garnish with the parsley. Using a vegetable peeler or a cheese plane, cut shavings from the Parmesan wedge over each crostino. Serve at once.

Serve with a slightly spicy, medium-bodied Syrah or your favourite cocktails.

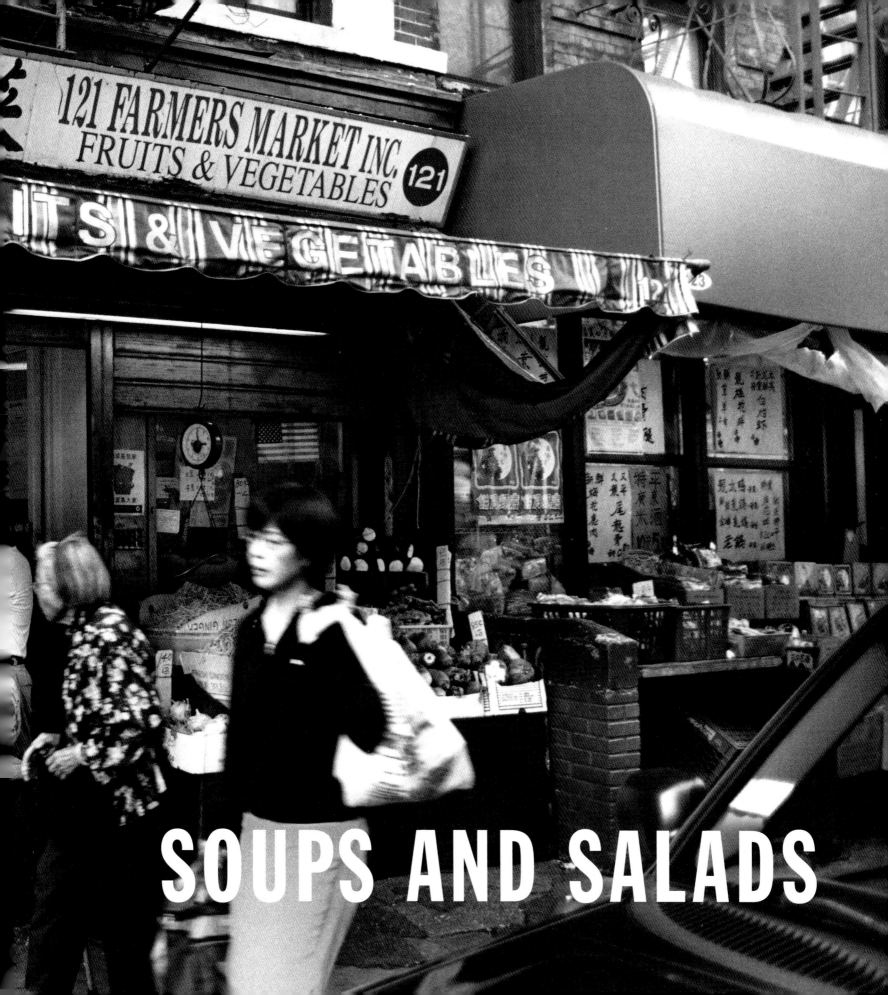

SOUPS AND SALADS

Among the repertoire of beloved soups and salads, some are the inspired

seasonal creations of local chefs, others the contributions of immigrants.

New Yorkers are no-nonsense when it comes to soups and salads. They have a special affinity for standbys connected with culinary history: the wedge of iceberg lettuce with tangy blue cheese dressing served at traditional steak houses, the matzo ball soup from a renowned deli, and the classic chowder made with local clams. Soups and salads lend themselves to bold presentations of seasonal ingredients, such as lobster and avocado salad in summer and butternut squash and apple soup in autumn. Cuban bean soup and Russian borscht reflect the ethnic influences that pervade the city's cuisine.

MANHATTAN CLAM CHOWDER

People have strong preferences for either the New England creamy clam chowder or the Manhattan tomato-based version. Credit for inventing the chunky soup probably goes to early French immigrants to Canada. Some believe Rhode Islanders were the first to add tomatoes, others that the Manhattan version descended from chowders sold at Coney Island food stands. A likelier possibility is that it was the creation of fish-monger William H. Winters, who owned the original Fulton Fish Market in the early 1900s. This recipe is from native New Yorker Rick Moonen, of restaurant RM. Cockles can be substituted for clams.

1 Place the quahog or littleneck clams in a wide saucepan, discarding any that do not close to the touch. Add 500 ml (16 fl oz) water, bring to the boil over high heat, cover, and steam just until the clams open, 8–10 minutes. Transfer the clams to a bowl, discarding any that failed to open, and reserve the clam cooking liquid in the pot. When the clams are cool enough to touch, remove the meat and chop, then set aside. Strain the clam liquid through a double layer of muslin and set aside.

2 In a soup pot over high heat, fry the bacon, stirring occasionally, until lightly browned, 5–6 minutes. Add the onion and garlic, reduce the heat to low and cook, stirring occasionally, until the onion is translucent, about 5 minutes. Add the celery, carrots, bay leaf, thyme, oregano, basil, and dried chilli flakes and cook until the vegetables begin to soften, about 5 minutes. Add the tomatoes, return to a simmer, and cook until they break down, about 10 minutes. Add the potatoes, clam juice and reserved clam liquid, return to a simmer, and cook until the potatoes are just tender, 8–10 minutes. Taste the soup and adjust

the seasoning with salt and pepper. (The soup can be prepared up to this point, cooled to room temperature, and refrigerated for up to 1 day. Refrigerate the reserved chopped clams separately. Before serving, reheat the soup gently over medium heat.)

3 Just before serving, add the bay scallops and the Manila clams in their shells, discarding any that do not close to the touch. Cook over medium heat until the clams open and the scallops are opaque, 4–5 minutes. Discard any clams that failed to open, and stir in the 10 g (⅓ oz) parsley and reserved chopped clams. Do not allow the soup to simmer or the clams will toughen. Stir in the lemon juice to taste.

4 Divide the chowder among warmed individual bowls, making sure that each portion includes whole clams and scallops. Garnish with parsley. Serve at once.

Serve with a spicy, light red wine, such as an Australian Shiraz.

12 quahog clams or 18–24 little-neck or cherrystone clams, well scrubbed

6 rashers bacon, chopped

1 large yellow onion, diced

4 cloves garlic, chopped

3 celery stalks, finely diced

2 carrots, peeled and finely diced

1 bay leaf

1 teaspoon *each* dried thyme, oregano, and basil

¼ teaspoon dried chilli flakes

440 g (14 oz) canned whole peeled tomatoes, drained and crushed

375 g (¾ lb) russet potatoes, peeled and diced

180 ml (6 fl oz) bottled clam juice

Sea salt and freshly ground black pepper

125 g (¼ lb) bay scallops, off the shell, muscles removed

20–22 Manila clams, well scrubbed

10 g (⅓ oz) finely chopped fresh flat-leaf parsley, plus more for garnish

1–2 tablespoons fresh lemon juice

Makes 6 servings

LOBSTER AND AVOCADO SALAD

Until 1910, when lobster chowder meant for the servants was accidentally served to the John D. Rockefeller family at their summer home in Maine, the rich, buttery crustacean was not considered a delicacy. Lobster from Maine is the most abundant type enjoyed on the eastern seaboard, but Montauk, at the eastern tip of Long Island, is a great source for local lobster and the home of lobster fishermen since colonial days. New York chefs serve mayonnaise-based lobster salad on its own or stuffed into toasted, buttered rolls. This light version is tossed in citrus juice and olive oil and enriched with avocado.

2 live lobsters, about 750 g (1½ lb) each, or 500 g (1 lb) fresh, cooked, chilled lobster meat

1 fennel bulb

10 fresh mint leaves

1 red onion, cut into very thin half-moon slices

1 clove garlic, finely chopped

2 tablespoons finely chopped fresh flat-leaf parsley

125 ml (4 fl oz) extra-virgin olive oil, plus 2 tablespoons

Juice of ½ orange

Grated zest and juice of 1 lemon

Sea salt and freshly ground pepper

250 g (½ lb) lamb's lettuce or baby rocket

1 ripe but firm avocado, peeled and diced

375 g (12 oz) cherry tomatoes, halved

Makes 6 servings

1 Bring a large pot three-quarters full of water to the boil over high heat. Using tongs, immerse the lobsters head-first in the boiling water. Cover and cook for about 8 minutes. Uncover, lift out the lobsters with the tongs, and set on a work surface. When the lobsters are cool enough to handle, snap the 2 large claws off each lobster and remove any rubber bands or pegs. Using a small, sharp knife, make a lengthways cut along the underside of each lobster. Remove and discard the small intestine in the centre of the tail and the sand sac and coral from the head. Using a lobster cracker or mallet, gently crack the claws. Remove the meat from the tail and claws and roughly chop into bite-sized pieces. Place in a bowl, cover and refrigerate until chilled, at least 1 hour or up to overnight.

2 Cut off the stems and feathery leaves from the fennel bulb and discard. Discard the outer layer of the bulb if it is tough and cut away any discoloured areas. Quarter the bulb lengthways and cut away any tough base portions. Cut the fennel quarters horizontally into very thin slices. Stack the mint leaves, roll them into a cylinder, and then cut the cylinder horizontally to make thin strips. In a large bowl, combine the fennel slices, mint strips, chilled lobster meat, onion, garlic, parsley, 125 ml (4 fl oz) olive oil, orange juice, lemon zest, and half of the lemon juice. Season to taste with salt and pepper and toss gently to combine.

3 Place the lamb's lettuce in a bowl, add the avocado and tomatoes, drizzle with the 2 tablespoons olive oil and the remaining lemon juice and toss gently to coat. Season to taste with salt and pepper.

4 Divide the lamb's lettuce, avocado, and tomatoes among individual plates. Top with the lobster salad, dividing evenly, and serve at once.

Serve with a white wine such as a Chardonnay or white Bordeaux.

MIXED GREEN SALAD WITH BEETS, GREEN BEANS, AND GOAT CHEESE

Beetroot is popular during the summer when many varieties and colours, such as golden beetroot and pink-and-white-striped Chioggia beetroot, appear in local farmers' markets. New York cooks toss cooked beetroot with fresh herbs or sliced fennel, or pair it with pungent or tangy cheeses, such as blue cheese or goat's cheese. Roasting the beetroot caramelises them to bring out their sweet flavour. A fresh cheese such as the goat's cheese from Coach Farm in the Hudson River Valley would be ideal for sprinkling on this salad.

1 Preheat the oven to 200°C (400°F). If the beetroot tops are still attached, cut them off, leaving 2.5 cm (1 inch) of the stem attached to avoid piercing the skin (leave the root attached as well). Save the tops for another use. Put the beetroot in a baking dish with water to a depth of 6 mm (¼ inch). Cover and bake until the beetroot are easily pierced with the tip of a knife, about 1 hour. Remove from the oven and, when cool enough to handle, peel the beetroot and trim the roots, then set aside to cool completely. Cut the beetroot into 6-mm (¼-inch) cubes. Set aside.

2 Meanwhile, bring a saucepan three-quarters full of salted water to the boil over high heat. Add the French beans or mangetout and cook until tender-crisp, 4–7 minutes; the timing will depend on their size. Drain and immerse in a bowl of ice water. Drain and set aside.

3 To make the vinaigrette, in a small bowl, whisk together the shallot, sugar, sherry vinegar, and mustard. Whisking constantly, add the olive oil in a thin, steady stream, then the rapeseed oil. Season to taste with salt and pepper.

4 Place the mixed greens and French beans in a large bowl. Drizzle with all but about 2 tablespoons of the vinaigrette and toss to coat. Divide the greens and beans among individual salad plates. Top with the cubed beetroot, dividing evenly, and drizzle with the remaining vinaigrette. Crumble the goat's cheese over the salads, again dividing evenly, and serve at once. Serve with a dry cider.

4–6 small golden, Chioggia or red beetroot, about 450 g (1 lb) total weight

Sea salt

450 g (1 lb) French beans, ends trimmed, or mangetouts, ends and strings removed

FOR THE VINAIGRETTE

1 shallot, finely chopped

1 teaspoon sugar

3 tablespoons sherry vinegar

1 teaspoon Dijon mustard

2 tablespoons extra-virgin olive oil

2 tablespoons rapeseed oil

Sea salt and freshly ground pepper

315 g (10 oz) mixed baby greens such as oakleaf lettuce, rocket, dandelion, mizuna, radicchio and/or sorrel

125 g (¼ lb) fresh goat's cheese, at room temperature

Makes 6 servings

Chefs at the Greenmarket

New York's best chefs are dedicated to using seasonal ingredients from local sources. In the dewy, early morning hours, chefs in their whites wander through the Union Square Greenmarket, the largest of the thirty farmers' markets in the city and the hub of New York's food scene. Rather than have fruit and vegetables delivered to their back doors, they come to the market themselves to scout around for the week's new arrivals: asparagus and rampions in May; cherries and sweetcorn in July; and plums and tomatoes in August. The rewards of their foraging are featured in "market menus" at restaurants such as Craft, Union Square Café, and Tocqueville.

Regulars at the Greenmarket include Peter Hoffman of Savoy loading up his bicycle with produce from Keith's Farm and Maury Rubin carrying a crate of Ronnybrook Farm Dairy cream back to City Bakery. Colin Alevras of The Tasting Room can be spotted selecting fresh scallops and lobster from Long Island's Blue Moon. The chefs' patronage alone cannot support the farmers, but their custom increases public awareness of the markets and the region's producers.

CUBAN BLACK BEAN SOUP

Cubans are the second-largest Hispanic population in New York, after Puerto Ricans. Cuban and Cuban-Chinese (an odd but historically justified combination) restaurants have long been ladling out bowls of thick, rich black bean soup. The traditional soup is even a signature dish of Douglas Rodriguez — one the most influential Latino chefs in the nation – who introduced his self-styled Nuevo Latino cuisine, including dishes from his native Cuba, to New Yorkers in 1994. Integral to the soup is sofrito, *a mixture that consists of onions, garlic, sweet peppers, chillies, herbs, spices, and sometimes ham.*

440 g (14 oz) dried black beans

2 bay leaves

FOR THE *SOFRITO*

180 ml (6 fl oz) extra-virgin olive oil

2 red sweet peppers, seeded and chopped

2 large white onions, chopped

8 cloves garlic, chopped

2 tablespoons dried oregano

1½ tablespoons ground cumin

Sea salt

1 tablespoon sugar

1 tablespoon sherry vinegar, or more to taste

2 tablespoons dry sherry, or more to taste

1 red onion, finely diced, for garnish

15 g (½ oz) fresh coriander leaves, for garnish

Makes 6 servings

1 Pick over the beans, discarding any misshapen beans or grit. Rinse the beans well, put them in a bowl and add water to cover by about 7.5 cm (3 inches). Soak for at least 4 hours or up to overnight. (Alternatively, for a quick soak, bring the beans and water to a rapid simmer and cook for 2 minutes. Remove from the heat, cover and let stand for 1 hour.) Drain the beans and place in a large soup pot with the bay leaves and 4 l (6 pts 8 fl oz) water. Bring to the boil over high heat, reduce the heat to low and simmer, stirring occasionally and adding more water if the beans become exposed, until the beans are tender, about 2 hours.

2 Meanwhile, make the *sofrito:* In a large sauté pan over medium heat, warm the olive oil. Add the sweet peppers and cook until they begin to soften, about 5 minutes. Add the white onions and cook until tender and translucent, 10–12 minutes. Add the garlic, oregano, cumin, and 1½ tablespoons salt and cook until the garlic is fragrant, about 2 minutes longer. Remove from the heat and allow the *sofrito* to cool slightly. Transfer the mixture to a blender or food processor and purée until smooth, 2–3 minutes.

3 Stir the *sofrito* and sugar into the beans and simmer until all of the flavours are combined, 20–30 minutes. Stir in the 1 tablespoon vinegar and 2 tablespoons dry sherry. Taste the soup and adjust the seasoning with vinegar, dry sherry, and salt. Serve the soup warm, ladled into bowls and garnished with the diced red onion and the coriander leaves.

Serve with a small glass of sweet cream sherry.

TRUFFLED WALDORF SALAD

Oscar Tschirky, a maitre d'hôtel at Manhattan's Waldorf-Astoria, is credited with inventing the Waldorf salad in 1893. The combination of apples, celery, and mayonnaise became an iconic item on the hotel's luncheon menu. As the popularity of the salad spread, walnuts were incorporated into the crunchy mix. To this day, the original salad is still served at the hotel. But at the hotel's bistro, Oscar's American Brasserie, chef John Doherty substitutes celeriac for the celery and adds truffle oil to the dressing for a contemporary version.

1 To make the dressing, in a large bowl, whisk together the sour cream, mayonnaise, yoghurt, lemon juice, and truffle oil. Season to taste with salt.

2 Preheat the oven to 180°C (350°F). Spread the walnut pieces on a baking sheet and toast until fragrant and lightly browned, about 10 minutes. Pour on to a plate, let cool, then coarsely chop. Set aside.

3 Using a small, sharp knife, peel away the rough skin from the celeriac. With the knife, cut the celeriac into slices 3 mm (⅛ inch) thick. Stack the slices and cut them into matchsticks. Add the celeriac to the dressing and toss to coat. Slice the cored apples horizontally into slices 3 mm (⅛ inch) thick. Stack the slices and cut into matchsticks. Add the apples to the celeriac and dressing and toss to coat.

4 Arrange 3 chicory leaves on each individual plate. Top with the apple mixture, dividing evenly, and sprinkle with the toasted walnuts. Serve at once.

Serve with a spicy, fruity Gewürztraminer.

FOR THE DRESSING

250 ml (8 fl oz) sour cream

180 ml (6 fl oz) mayonnaise

185 ml (6 fl oz) natural yoghurt

Juice of 2 lemons

1 teaspoon white truffle oil

Sea salt

125 g (4 oz) walnut pieces

1 celeriac, about 185 g (6 oz)

2 Granny Smith or other tart green apples, cored

2 Red Delicious or other sweet red apples, cored

1 head chicory (witloof), leaves separated, about 24 leaves total

Makes 8 servings

New York Originals

Whether the field is art or architecture, fashion, or food, New York is where people look to discover what's new. The city's notable culinary innovations include its having been home to the first dedicated restaurant in the United States. Delmonico's scored another first soon after it opened in 1830 by creating the world's first à la carte menu.

Several classic dishes emerged from Delmonico's kitchen. Lobster Newberg was prepared for a sea captain, and baked Alaska, though variations already existed, was christened at the restaurant to commemorate the newly acquired territory. Legend has it that the Benedicts, dedicated patrons, deserve credit, along with the chef, for adding eggs Benedict to the menu. English muffins, often the foundation for eggs Benedict, were also invented in New York (it was the baker, not the muffin, that was English).

Choice of name is especially confusing in the case of the egg cream, which contains neither eggs nor cream. The foaming drink of milk, chocolate syrup, and soda water was invented at a Brooklyn soda fountain in the late 1800s. The name itself remains a mystery.

BEEF, BEET, AND CABBAGE BORSCHT

Recipes for borscht have always varied, depending on their origin — Ukraine, Poland, or Russia — as well as the cook's preferences. Some borschts are a cornucopia of vegetables; contemporary versions might use chicken stock rather than beef, or even be vegetarian. This soup begins with a rich broth made from beef marrow bones, which is customary in eastern European cooking. Borscht is a staple at Jewish delis and dairies, at boardwalk restaurants in Brooklyn's Brighton Beach, and at Veselka, a Ukrainian diner in the East Village, which ladles out hot or cold borscht twenty-four hours a day.

FOR THE SOUP

1.5 kg (3 lb) beef marrow bones

Sea salt

1.25 kg (2½ lb) brisket, trimmed of excess fat

440 g (14 oz) canned whole plum tomatoes

1 large yellow onion, quartered

2 celery stalks, cut into 15-cm (6-inch) pieces

1 teaspoon black peppercorns

1 fresh bay leaf

750 g (1½ lb) red beetroot

90 ml (3½ fl oz) apple cider vinegar, or to taste

Sea salt and freshly ground pepper

½ small green cabbage, thinly sliced, about 185 g (6 oz)

½ large yellow onion, diced

1 celery stalk, diced

2 carrots, peeled and thinly sliced

2 tablespoons chopped fresh dill, plus more for garnish

1 tablespoon sugar, or to taste

Sour cream for garnish

Makes 10–12 servings

1 Place the bones in a large soup pot with 4 l (6 pts 8 fl oz) water and 1 tablespoon salt. Bring to the boil over high heat, reduce the heat to low, cover partially and simmer, frequently skimming the foam that rises to the surface, about 1 hour. Carefully remove the bones from the pot and discard. Add the brisket, tomatoes and their liquid, onion, celery, peppercorns, and bay leaf. Bring to the boil over high heat, reduce the heat to low, cover partially and simmer until the brisket is fork-tender, about 2 hours.

2 Transfer the brisket to a bowl. Strain the liquid into a separate bowl, pressing on the solids with the back of a spoon to extract all the liquid. Discard the solids. Cover the brisket and liquid and refrigerate until the liquid is chilled, at least 4 hours or up to overnight.

3 If the greens are still attached to the beetroot, remove them. Cut the beetroot into halves or quarters. Bring a saucepan containing 2 l (3½ pts) water to the boil over high heat. Add the beetroot, 2 tablespoons apple cider vinegar, and 1 tablespoon salt; cover and return to the boil, then reduce the heat to medium-low and simmer the beetroot until very tender, about 1 hour, adding more water if necessary to cover it. Let the beetroot cool in its cooking liquid.

4 Skim the fat from the surface of the chilled beef soup and pour into a pot placed over medium heat. Cut the meat into 6-mm (¼-inch) cubes, add to the soup and heat until warm, about 10 minutes. Add the cabbage, onion, and celery and simmer until tender, about 20 minutes.

5 Remove the beetroot from its cooking liquid and strain the liquid into the soup pot. Slip off the skins and grate the beetroot on the large holes of a box grater-shredder. Add the grated beetroot to the soup pot with the carrots and 2 tablespoons dill. Simmer over medium-low heat until the carrots are tender, about 15 minutes. Stir in the vinegar and 1 tablespoon sugar and season to taste with salt and pepper. Taste the soup and add vinegar and/or sugar if necessary.

6 Ladle the borscht into warmed individual soup bowls. Garnish each bowl with a dollop of sour cream and a sprinkling of dill. Serve at once.

ICEBERG WEDGES WITH BLUE CHEESE DRESSING

Iceberg lettuce, also called crisphead lettuce, was developed in Doylestown, Pennsylvania, more than a century ago. In recent years, the salads of iceberg, once ubiquitous on restaurant menus, have been supplanted by those of mixed lettuces and other tender greens. But the wedge of iceberg garnished with a thick, luscious blue cheese dressing remains dear to the hearts of New Yorkers. Ordering the salad at steakhouses such as The Palm, Keen's, Peter Luger's, and Smith and Wollensky is a tradition.

1 In a small bowl, whisk together the mayonnaise, sour cream, lemon juice, Tabasco, ¼ teaspoon salt, and ¼ teaspoon pepper. Stir in the blue cheese and 3 tablespoons chives. Taste the dressing and adjust the seasoning with salt, if desired.

2 Using a small, sharp knife, cut away the core from the head of lettuce. Remove and discard the outer leaves if they are limp or blemished. Cut the head into 6 uniform wedges.

3 Place each wedge on a chilled individual plate. Spoon a generous amount of the dressing over each wedge, dividing it evenly. You may not need all of the dressing. Garnish with chives and serve at once.

Serve with a light, slightly spicy, fruity red such as Cabernet Franc.

125 ml (4 fl oz) mayonnaise

125 ml (4 fl oz) sour cream

Juice of 1 lemon

Dash of Tabasco sauce

Sea salt and freshly ground pepper

185 g (6 oz) blue cheese, crumbled

3 tablespoons finely chopped fresh chives, plus slivers of chives for garnish

1 head iceberg (crisphead) lettuce, chilled

Makes 6 servings

New York Steakhouses

"New York steakhouse" refers to a very specific type of restaurant. The décor is dark wood, with white or chequered tablecloths. High-quality, aged steaks anchor the menu, which also features such first courses as a wedge of iceberg lettuce with blue cheese dressing and sliced beefsteak tomatoes and onions. Standard accompaniments include creamed spinach and fried, mashed, or jacket potatoes. The star of the dessert list is cheesecake.

The steakhouse has a long tradition. One of the earliest was Old Homestead, still in its original location in the Meatpacking District. When the restaurant opened in 1868, the district was on the outskirts of town where farmers brought their cattle to market. Two venerable steakhouses followed: Keens, in the Garment District, in 1885, and Peter Luger, in Brooklyn, in 1887. The tradition firmly took hold in the 1920s with two famed institutions, Gallagher's, started by a Ziegfeld Follies dancer, and The Palm. A new generation of steakhouses, including Jean-Georges Vongerichten's V Steakhouse and Laurent Tourondel's BLT Steak, offers creative reinventions of classic recipes.

CHICKEN MATZO BALL SOUP

Traditionally served for Passover, chicken matzo ball soup is now eaten throughout the year. Its popularity has gained it a place in the pantheon of New York food. Two elements are crucial: the broth and the matzo balls themselves. The broth should be golden, rich and strongly flavoured. The matzo balls need to float rather than sink in the soup. There is no better example than at the Second Avenue Deli, on the Lower East Side, which is famous for its light, tender matzo balls. This soup is best made a day in advance so that the fat skimmed from the cold broth can be used to make the matzo balls.

1 chicken, 2–2.5 kg (4–5 lb), preferably a boiling fowl

6 chicken wings

10 g (⅓ oz) fresh flat-leaf parsley leaves, plus 10 g (⅓ oz) chopped flat-leaf parsley

10 g (⅓ oz) fresh dill, plus 3 tablespoons chopped dill

½ teaspoon peppercorns

1 large yellow onion

1 turnip

5 large carrots

3 celery stalks

1 clove garlic

2 bay leaves

Sea salt and freshly ground pepper

4 large eggs

60 ml (2 fl oz) reserved chicken fat or rapeseed oil

140 g (4½ oz) matzo meal

90 g (3 oz) sliced leeks, white and pale green parts only

Juice of ½ lemon

Makes 6–8 servings

1 To make the broth, remove the giblets and neck from the chicken cavity and reserve for another use or discard. Rinse the chicken and put it in a large soup pot along with the chicken wings. Place the 10 g (⅓ oz) parsley leaves, 10 g (⅓ oz) dill, and the peppercorns on a 10-cm (4-inch) square of muslin, bring up the corners and tie together with kitchen string to make a bouquet garni. Peel and quarter the onion and turnip. Scrape 2 of the carrots and cut each into 4 equal pieces. Cut 2 of the celery stalks into 4 equal pieces. Add the bouquet garni, onion, turnip, carrots, celery, garlic, bay leaves, and 1 tablespoon sea salt to the pot along with 4.5 l (7 pts 4 fl oz) water. Bring to the boil over high heat, reduce the heat to low, cover partially and simmer, frequently skimming the foam that rises to the surface, until the chicken is tender, about 1½ hours. Carefully remove the whole chicken from the broth using long-handled tongs. Set aside to cool.

2 Continue to simmer the vegetables and chicken wings, partially covered, until you have a rich soup, about 2 hours longer. Strain the soup and discard the solids. Allow the soup to cool to room temperature, then cover and refrigerate overnight. The next day, skim the fat from the top and, if desired, reserve for making the matzo balls.

3 When the chicken has cooled, remove and discard the skin. Pull the meat from the bones and discard the bones. Shred the meat into bite-sized pieces. Cover and refrigerate until ready to use.

4 To make the matzo balls, in a large bowl beat the eggs well with a whisk. Add the reserved chicken fat or rapeseed oil, 60 ml (2 fl oz) of the soup, 1 tablespoon of the chopped dill, 1 teaspoon salt, and ½ teaspoon pepper and beat to combine. Using a wooden spoon, stir in the matzo meal until well blended. Cover the dough and refrigerate for 1 hour.

5 Bring a large pot three-quarters full of water to the boil over high heat. Reduce the heat to a simmer and stir in 3 tablespoons salt. With damp hands, form the matzo dough into balls about 2.5 cm (1 inch) in diameter, periodically running your hands under cold water to prevent the dough from sticking. You should have enough dough to make about 16 matzo balls. Carefully slip the balls, one at a time, into the boiling water. Cover and gently boil the matzo balls until they have more than doubled in size, about 30 minutes.

6 Meanwhile, reheat the soup over medium heat. Season to taste with salt and pepper. Peel and dice the remaining 3 carrots. Dice the remaining celery stalk. Add to the soup along with the reserved chicken meat, sliced leeks and the chopped parsley. Simmer until the vegetables are tender, 30 minutes. Just before serving, add the remaining 2 tablespoons chopped dill and the lemon juice.

7 To serve, place 2 or 3 matzo balls in each bowl, ladle the soup into the bowls, and serve at once.

Serve with a robust Chardonnay.

BUTTERNUT SQUASH AND APPLE SOUP WITH FRIED SAGE

Autumn is New York's finest season and nowhere is this more apparent than in the farmers' markets around the city. The last of the plums gives way to bunches of fragrant Concord grapes and crates of just-picked apples. Sweetcorn and tomatoes are replaced by winter squash – acorn, butternut, and Hubbard – piled high on tables in all their glorious shapes, colours, and sizes. New Yorkers are ready to savour hearty, warming flavours such as this puréed soup combining the season's apples and squash.

1 Preheat the oven to 220°C (425°F). Place the squash and apples on a rimmed baking sheet. Drizzle with 3 tablespoons of the olive oil, season with salt and pepper, toss to coat and spread out in a single layer. Roast until the squash and apples are tender and light brown in places, 30–40 minutes.

2 In a medium soup pot over medium heat, warm the remaining 2 tablespoons oil. Add the onion, carrots, and celery and cook, stirring often, until the onion is translucent and the carrots and celery are soft, 10–15 minutes. Add the shallots and garlic and cook for 1 minute. Add the squash, apples, vinegar, chicken stock, and finely chopped sage. Bring to the boil, reduce the heat to low, and simmer for 30 minutes to let the flavours mingle.

3 Meanwhile, to make the fried sage, in a small frying pan over medium-high heat, melt the butter with the olive oil. Add the sage leaves, a few at a time, and fry until barely crisp, about 1 minute. (The leaves will crisp further when removed from the pan.) Transfer to kitchen towels to drain.

4 Using a blender or a food processor, purée the soup until smooth. Return the soup to the pot, if necessary, and add the remaining 500 ml (16 fl oz) stock if the soup is too thick. Warm over medium-low heat. Taste and adjust the seasoning with salt and pepper. Ladle into warmed individual bowls, crumble the sage over the top, drizzle with crème fraîche and serve at once.

Serve with a fruity Riesling.

1 butternut squash, about 750 g (1½ lb), peeled, seeded and cut into 2.5-cm (1-inch) cubes

3 sweet apples such as Pink Lady or McIntosh, peeled, cored, and chopped

75 ml (2½ fl oz) olive oil

Sea salt and freshly ground pepper

½ large yellow onion, diced

2 small carrots, peeled and diced

2 celery stalks, diced

2 shallots, finely chopped

2 cloves garlic, finely chopped

1 teaspoon apple cider vinegar

1.1–2 l (2–3½ pts) chicken stock

6 fresh sage leaves, finely chopped

FOR THE FRIED SAGE

2 tablespoons unsalted butter

2 tablespoons olive oil

18 whole fresh sage leaves

Crème fraîche or double cream for garnish

Makes 6 servings

New York Apples

Partly due to the city's nickname, the Big Apple, New York State is often associated with apples, though the moniker really has nothing to do with the fruit. Nevertheless, apple-farming in the state dates back to the 1640s, when governor Peter Stuyvesant planted a tree from Holland on what is now Third Avenue. The idea caught on, and in the 1700s colonists grew apples for cider, which was used as currency. Cultivation soon spread to the Hudson River Valley and Long Island, and the apple became New York's number-one fruit crop.

Hundreds of varieties originated in the state. Many popular apples go back centuries, such as the Newtown Pippin, dating to 1758, the Northern Spy to 1800, and the Jonathan to 1826. Others are recent creations: the Spigold, a cross between the Spy and the Golden Delicious, was introduced in 1962; the Jonamac, combining attributes of the Jonathan and the McIntosh, appeared in 1972. Many farmers prefer to plant lesser-known "antique" varieties, such as Golden Russet, Northern Spy, and Black Twig, which are available only at local farmers' markets.

MAIN COURSES

Main dishes can be as straightforward as a grilled New York steak

or as elegant as Long Island duck bathed in an orange sauce.

Comfort is the common denominator of main dishes, from a succulent brisket to herb-crusted lamb and crisp-skinned chicken, accompanied by delicious vegetable purées. Relatively simple fare is elevated by the use of the finest ingredients. Fresh mozzarella cheese from a local producer enriches baked ziti, a classic from the Italian-American kitchen, and quinces and apples from the farmers' market dress up braised pork. Nearby waters are the source of fresh seafood, whether skate or soft-shelled crabs. New York chefs are passionate about transforming even the humble hamburger into an unforgettable masterpiece.

NEW YORK STEAK WITH BEER-BATTERED ONION RINGS

In 1850, the famed restaurant Delmonico's served what is reputed to be the first steak in New York. The cut, a boneless rib-eye from the top loin, is most often referred to by New Yorkers as a strip steak. It is also known as New York steak and even Delmonico's steak. Whatever the name, it is now a classic that comes topped with herbed butter and crisp onion rings, and is served across the nation. It is typically ordered à la carte, with a green vegetable and perhaps a side dish of Delmonico's potatoes, boiled and dressed with butter, salt, and parsley.

1 To make the butter, in a small bowl, cream the butter with a wooden spoon. Stir in the herbs and ½ teaspoon each of salt and pepper. Cover tightly with clingfilm and refrigerate.

2 To make the steaks, prepare a charcoal or gas barbecue for direct grilling over high heat or preheat a cast-iron grill pan over medium-high heat. Season the steaks on both sides with salt and pepper, rubbing the seasonings into the meat, and brush both sides with olive oil. Place the steaks over the hottest part of the fire and sear on both sides, about 2 minutes per side, then grill, turning once, 6–8 minutes longer for rare, and 10–12 minutes for medium. If using a cast-iron grill pan, cook the steaks for 12 minutes for rare, and about 14 minutes for medium, turning once halfway through cooking. Transfer the steaks to a platter, tent with aluminium foil, and let rest for about 5 minutes.

3 Meanwhile, to make the onion rings, pour rape-seed oil into a large heavy-bottomed saucepan to reach a depth of 7.5–10 cm (3–4 inches). Heat the oil to 190°C (375°F) on a deep-frying thermometer. In a bowl, whisk together the flour and beer. Separate the onion slices into rings. While the steaks are resting, dip each onion ring into the batter, letting the excess drip back into the bowl. Working in batches to avoid crowding the pan, fry the rings until golden brown, 2–3 minutes. Using tongs, transfer to kitchen towels to drain. Sprinkle with salt.

4 Place each steak on a warmed individual plate, top with 1 tablespoon of the butter and mound with the onion rings, dividing evenly. Serve at once.

Serve with a full-bodied claret or red burgundy.

*Strip or New York steak is an American cut of boned rib of beef which is not a standard cut in the UK. The closest equivalent is a sirloin steak but you may be able to get your butcher to bone a rib or ribs for you.

FOR THE BUTTER

90 g (3 oz) unsalted butter, at cool room temperature

1½ tablespoons finely chopped fresh herbs such as rosemary, tarragon, thyme, marjoram, chives, and/or flat-leaf parsley

Sea salt and freshly ground pepper

FOR THE STEAKS

6 strip steaks*, each about 4 cm (1½ inches) thick, at room temperature

Sea salt and freshly ground pepper

Extra-virgin olive oil for brushing

FOR THE ONION RINGS

Rapeseed oil for deep-frying

155 g (5 oz) plain flour

250 ml (8 fl oz) dark beer

2 sweet onions, sliced horizontally into slices about 9–12 mm (⅓–½ inch) thick

Sea salt

Makes 6 servings

LONG ISLAND DUCK WITH ORANGE SAUCE

The Four Seasons restaurant in Midtown Manhattan is legendary. The exceptional food sometimes takes a backseat to the famous clientele, from politicians and diplomats to authors and celebrities, and to the stunning rooms designed by renowned architects Philip Johnson and Mies van der Rohe. Tree branches in the room change with the seasons, as does the roast duck, a house speciality, which is carved at the table and served each season with a different sauce. Preparation of the recipe needs to begin three days ahead, but is easier than you might think. Still, you might want to reserve this dish for a special occasion.

1 Long Island or Peking duck, 2–3 kg (4–6 lb), with neck and giblets

2 oranges

250 ml (8 fl oz) soy sauce

2.5-cm (1-inch) piece fresh ginger, peeled and cut into thin rounds

2 cloves garlic, halved

2 tablespoons honey

1½ teaspoons peppercorns

FOR THE ORANGE SAUCE

3 celery stalks, chopped

1 carrot, peeled and chopped

1 yellow onion, skin on, chopped

500 ml (16 fl oz) red wine

2 tablespoons tomato purée

1½ teaspoons plain flour

500 ml (16 fl oz) chicken stock

2 tablespoons orange marmalade

250 ml (8 fl oz) orange juice

2 tablespoons Grand Marnier

1 tablespoon red wine vinegar

Sea salt and freshly ground pepper

Makes 4 servings

1 Three days before serving the duck, remove the giblets and neck from the cavity and reserve for the sauce. Remove and discard any excess fat from the cavities. Rinse the duck and pat dry with kitchen towels. Cut off the wings and reserve with the giblets and neck. Using a small knife, make 6-mm (¼-inch) slits in the back of the duck, spacing them 2.5 cm (1 inch) apart and taking care not to puncture the flesh. Place a wire rack on a baking sheet, set the duck on the rack, and refrigerate, uncovered, to dry for 2 days.

2 Two days before serving the duck, zest 1 orange and set aside. Cut a slice off the top and bottom of each orange. Stand each orange upright on a cutting board. Following the contour of each orange and rotating it with each cut, slice downwards to remove the peel, pith and membrane. Cut the sections free from the membrane and place in a bowl. Cover and refrigerate the orange sections until needed. Stir together the zest, soy sauce, ginger, garlic, honey, and peppercorns to make a marinade. Cover and refrigerate overnight.

3 One day before serving the duck, place it breast side up in a large, shallow roasting tin. Strain the chilled marinade. Brush the duck with half of the marinade. Let it stand at room temperature for 20 minutes, then brush with the remaining marinade. Refrigerate the duck, uncovered, overnight.

4 The day the duck will be served, make the orange sauce: Preheat the oven to 200°C (400°F). Place the reserved neck, wings, giblets, and the celery, carrot and onion in a roasting tin and roast until the duck parts are deep brown, about 20 minutes. Transfer the

duck parts and vegetables to a saucepan. Place the roasting pan over medium heat, add 250 ml (8 fl oz) of the red wine and stir to scrape up any browned bits. Add the tomato purée to the saucepan and cook, stirring, over medium heat until the purée begins to colour, about 1 minute. Stir in the flour and cook for about 3 minutes. Add the rest of the red wine, the contents of the roasting pan and the chicken stock and bring to a boil. Reduce the heat to low and simmer until reduced by half, 5–6 minutes. Strain and discard the solids. Set the sauce aside.

5 Remove the duck from the refrigerator 20 minutes before roasting. Arrange the oven racks so that one is in the centre and another is in the lowest position. Reduce the oven temperature to 190°C (375°F). Pour water into a large roasting pan to a depth of 6 mm (¼ inch) and place on the lower rack. Set the duck, breast side up, directly on the centre rack over the water-filled pan and roast until the skin is dark brown, 1½–2 hours. Transfer the duck to a serving platter. Tent with aluminium foil and let rest for 10–15 minutes.

6 Meanwhile, finish the orange sauce. In a pan over medium heat, combine the marmalade, orange juice, Grand Marnier, and vinegar. Simmer until reduced by half, about 10 minutes. Stir in the reserved sauce. Season to taste with salt and pepper.

7 Carve the duck and arrange on warmed individual plates. Spoon the sauce over and around the duck. Garnish with the orange sections and serve at once.

Serve with a spicy, full-bodied Zinfandel or Pinot Noir.

PORK BRAISED IN RIESLING WITH APPLE-QUINCE COMPOTE

Unlike many chefs who send employees to pick up their orders, Peter Hoffman of Savoy Restaurant is a well-known presence at farmers' markets. Pedalling a blue bicycle fitted with a sidecar, he loads up on seasonal produce that he intends to serve at the SoHo restaurant he opened in 1990. Come October, he eagerly awaits the imminent arrival of quinces. During their short season, he prepares the aromatic, tart fruits in a variety of ways, often pairing them with apples, as in this compote served with slow-cooked pork.

1 Place the pork pieces in a non-reactive bowl and season on all sides with salt and pepper. Cover and refrigerate overnight.

2 In a flameproof casserole or heavy saucepan with a lid, over medium-high heat, warm the olive oil. Add the pork and sear on all sides until deep brown, about 8 minutes. Transfer to a plate. Reduce the heat to medium. Add the onions and fry until lightly browned, 8–10 minutes. Add the garlic, cinnamon, thyme, parsley, and bay leaf and sauté until the garlic is fragrant, about 2 minutes. Add the Riesling and deglaze the pan, scraping up any browned bits on the pan bottom. Return the pork to the pan and add enough water so that the liquid comes to the top of the pork. Season with salt and pepper, reduce the heat to low, cover and simmer until the meat is tender, about 1½ hours. Add the carrots and calvados and simmer, covered, until the carrots are tender, 30 minutes longer. Stir in the vinegar and season with salt and pepper.

3 To make the compote, peel, core and cut the quinces and apples into 2.5-cm (1-inch) chunks. In a saucepan over medium heat, melt the butter. Add the onion and cook until translucent, 10–12 minutes. Add the quinces, apples, Riesling, and honey. Reduce the heat to low and cook until the fruit is soft, 30–35 minutes. Stir in the mustard and the lemon zest and season to taste with salt.

4 Divide the pan juices and pork pieces between warmed individual plates. Serve the compote on the side.

Serve with a dry Riesling or a Gewürztraminer.

1 kg (2¼ lb) boned pork shoulder, trimmed of excess fat and cut into 5-cm (2-inch) pieces

Sea salt and freshly ground pepper

125 ml (4 fl oz) olive oil

2 medium yellow onions, diced

6 cloves garlic

1 cinnamon stick

4 sprigs *each* fresh thyme and flat-leaf parsley

1 bay leaf

750 ml (24 fl oz) Riesling

2 carrots, peeled and diced

125 ml (4 fl oz) calvados

2 teaspoons Champagne vinegar, cider vinegar, or to taste

FOR THE COMPOTE

3 *each* quinces and tart red apples

60 g (2 oz) unsalted butter

1 large yellow onion, diced

250 ml (8 fl oz) Riesling

90 g (3 oz) honey

1 tablespoon Dijon mustard

Grated zest of 1 lemon

Makes 4–6 servings

Quince

Yellowish-green with a bumpy exterior and a downy coat, quince has a tannic taste and hard, grainy texture when eaten raw. Stewing, poaching, or baking transforms the fruit, giving it a subtle apple flavour and a fragrance reminiscent of apricot and vanilla. The quince was brought to the United States by European settlers. Its early popularity has waned and many people are unsure of how to cook quinces, but during their short autumn season, New York chefs can't get enough of them.

At one time, numerous Hudson River Valley apple farmers also grew quince, but today, Locust Grove Farm, a sixth-generation fruit farm north of the city, is one of the only vendors at New York's Greenmarkets that sells quinces. In mid-October, just before the season starts, the farm's Union Square stand is abuzz with customers, most of them chefs, ordering the fruit before it has been picked. Until December, when the supply ends, quinces appear on the best menus in town. They are turned into compotes and chutneys for savoury dishes such as pork and foie gras, and pastry chefs use them in cakes and pies.

VEAL MILANESE

Veal Milanese is a staple on New York menus, from pizzerias in the Bronx and family-run restaurants in Manhattan's Little Italy to elegant restaurants such as The Palm, the famed steakhouse that originated on New York's Upper East Side, and Mario Batali's Babbo Ristorante e Enoteca and Sant Ambroeus, both in Greenwich Village. This contemporary version is simplified for the home cook, using veal escalopes instead of the classic rib chops. The dish is freshened up with an accompaniment of peppery rocket and tomato salad. If you make the salad in the winter, when rocket is not in season, use coriander leaves.

4 veal escalopes, each about 6 mm (¼ inch) thick

Sea salt and freshly ground pepper

185 g (6 oz) fine dry breadcrumbs

60 g (2 oz) Parmesan cheese, freshly grated

2 tablespoons finely chopped fresh flat-leaf parsley

1 tablespoon dried oregano, crumbled

2 large eggs

155 g (5 oz) plain flour

155 g (5 oz) rocket leaves

185 g (6 oz) small sweet tomatoes, halved

Extra-virgin olive oil

Juice of ½ lemon

Olive oil for frying

60 g (2 oz) unsalted butter

Wedge of Parmesan cheese

1 lemon, cut into eighths

Makes 4 servings

1 Place each veal slice between sheets of clingfilm. Using a steak hammer or rolling pin, pound to a uniform thickness of 3 mm (⅛ inch). Season both sides with salt and pepper.

2 On a dinner plate, stir together the breadcrumbs, grated Parmesan, parsley, oregano, 1 teaspoon salt, and ½ teaspoon pepper. Crack the eggs into a shallow bowl and beat lightly. Pour the flour on another dinner plate. Dredge each veal slice in the flour, shaking off the excess, then dip into the beaten eggs, letting the excess drip back into the bowl. Finally, dredge in the breadcrumb mixture, pressing the crumbs onto both sides. Place the coated slices in a single layer on a tray or baking sheet. Cover with clingfilm and refrigerate until you are ready to cook the veal.

3 In a large bowl, combine the rocket and tomatoes. Drizzle with enough extra-virgin olive oil to coat the leaves lightly. Sprinkle with the lemon juice, season to taste with salt and pepper and gently toss. Set aside.

4 Heat a large, heavy frying pan over medium-high heat until very hot. Pour in enough olive oil to reach a depth of 6 mm (¼ inch) and add the butter. When the butter melts and the mixture is hot but not smoking, working in batches, place the coated veal slices in the pan; do not crowd the slices. Cook until golden brown, 1–2 minutes. Turn and cook on the second side until golden brown, 1–2 minutes longer. Transfer to kitchen towels to drain.

5 Divide the veal slices among warmed individual plates. Mound the salad alongside, dividing it evenly. Using a vegetable peeler or a cheese plane, cut 4 or 5 shavings from the Parmesan wedge over each salad. Place 2 lemon wedges on each plate and serve.

Serve with a soft, non-acidic Pinot Noir.

Variation: To make a classic veal Milanese, substitute 4 small veal rib chops for the escalopes. Pound each rib chop as described in step 1, leaving the rib bone attached. Proceed with the recipe as written.

BEEF BRISKET WITH SWEET POTATOES AND PRUNES

The Jewish Sabbath lasts from sundown on Friday until sundown on Saturday. Among traditional Sabbath observances is the prohibition on lighting a fire or cooking. Since brisket benefits from long, slow cooking, the meat for the Sabbath was placed in the oven by sundown on Friday and left to cook in the residual heat until the next day. Brisket with sweet potatoes and fruit, in this case, prunes, is called a tsimmes (TSIM-ez), referring to a number of ingredients cooked in one pot. The Yiddish word also means "fuss", as in "Don't make a tsimmes of it". Serve with egg noodles, noodle kugel or potato pancakes.

1 Trim the brisket of excess fat, then rinse and pat dry with kitchen towels. Rub the meat on all sides with the paprika and season generously with salt and black pepper. In a large flameproof casserole or other ovenproof pot with a lid over medium-high heat, warm 2 tablespoons of the oil. Add the brisket and sear on all sides until deep brown, about 4 minutes per side. Transfer to a plate and set aside.

2 Preheat the oven to 180°C (350°F). In the same flameproof casserole or pot over medium heat, warm the remaining 2 tablespoons oil. Add the onions and cook, stirring occasionally, until golden brown and tender, 10–15 minutes. Add the garlic, allspice and dried chilli flakes and sauté until the garlic is fragrant, about 2 minutes. Return the brisket to the pot, fat side up. Pour in the wine, tomatoes and 1 l (1¾ pints) water. Add the bay leaves and thyme and rosemary sprigs. Cover, place in the oven and cook, basting the meat often with the sauce in the pot, until the meat is tender and breaks apart easily when pierced with a fork, about 3 hours.

3 Remove from the oven, add the sweet potatoes, carrots, and plums. Cover and continue to cook until the sweet potatoes and carrots are soft, about 1 hour longer. Let the meat and vegetables cool in the sauce to room temperature, then refrigerate for at least 4 hours or up to overnight.

4 When you are ready to serve the brisket, preheat the oven to 180°C (350°F). Remove the pot from the refrigerator and skim the fat from the surface of the liquid. Transfer the meat to a cutting board and cut across the grain into slices 12 mm (½ inch) thick. Return the meat to the pot, cover, place in the oven and cook until the meat, vegetables, and sauce are heated through, about 30 minutes. Arrange the sliced brisket on a warmed platter with the vegetables and spoon the sauce over the top. Garnish with the parsley and serve at once.

Serve with a full-bodied Cabernet Sauvignon or other dry red wine from Israel or Rabbi Jacob from Morocco.

1 beef brisket, 2–2.5 kg (4–5 lb)

1 teaspoon Hungarian paprika

Sea salt and freshly ground black pepper

60 ml (2 fl oz) rapeseed oil

3 large yellow onions, chopped

4 cloves garlic, chopped

½ teaspoon ground allspice

¼ teaspoon dried chilli flakes

500 ml (16 fl oz) red wine

440 g (14 oz) canned tomatoes, crushed

2 bay leaves

2 sprigs fresh thyme

1 sprig fresh rosemary

1 kg (2 lb) orange-fleshed sweet potatoes, peeled and sliced horizontally into 2.5-cm (1-inch) rounds

6–8 small carrots, peeled and cut into 4-cm (1½-inch) pieces

250 g (½ lb) stoned prunes

10 g (⅓ oz) chopped fresh flat-leaf parsley for garnish

Makes 8 servings

RISOTTO WITH PEAS, MOREL MUSHROOMS, AND RAMPS

In May 1974, Sirio Maccioni, owner of Le Cirque restaurant (now Le Cirque 2000) and patriarch of one of New York's premier restaurant families, was travelling in Canada. Craving pasta, he turned to various vegetables in season for the sauce and called it Spaghetti Primavera. Craig Claiborne wrote about the pasta in the New York Times, *and customers began ordering it even though it was not on the menu. This risotto, an ode to that famous pasta, was invented by Maccioni's wife, Egi. It uses unusual springtime ingredients, including morel mushrooms and rampions, wild leeks with a strong, garlicky flavour.*

8 asparagus spears, trimmed, peeled if the skin is tough, and cut into slices 6 mm (¼ inch) thick

155 g (5 oz) garden peas

60 g (2 oz) pine nuts

125 g (¼ lb) morel or chestnut mushrooms, brushed clean, trimmed and halved lengthwise

90 g (3 oz) unsalted butter, cut into small pieces

3 tablespoons olive oil

1.5 l (2 pints 8 fl oz) chicken stock, or as needed

4 or 5 rampions, Welsh or spring onions, white part finely chopped and green tops thinly sliced

1 clove garlic, thinly sliced

450 g (I lb) Carnoroli, Arborio or Vialone Nano rice

375 ml (12 fl oz) dry white wine

15 g (½ oz) chopped fresh flat-leaf parsley leaves

185 g (6 oz) freshly grated Parmesan cheese, or as needed, plus more for serving

Sea salt and freshly ground pepper

Makes 4–6 servings

1 Bring a saucepan three-quarters full of water to the boil. Add the asparagus and blanch the slices for 1 minute. Using a slotted spoon, transfer to a bowl of ice water to halt the cooking. Drain and set aside. Repeat with the peas, blanching them for about 4 minutes. Set the vegetables aside.

2 Place the pine nuts in a heavy, dry frying pan over medium heat and toast, shaking the pan occasionally, until fragrant and golden, 5–7 minutes. Transfer to a plate and set aside.

3 If using morel mushrooms, immerse the halves in a bowl of water, stir vigorously with your fingers to dislodge any dirt and drain. Pat dry with kitchen towels. In a frying pan over medium heat, melt 2 tablespoons of the butter with 1 tablespoon of the olive oil. Add the mushrooms and sauté until tender, about 7 minutes. Remove from the heat and set aside.

4 Pour the chicken stock into a large saucepan over medium heat and bring to a simmer. Adjust the heat to maintain a gentle simmer.

5 In a large saucepan over medium heat, melt 2 tablespoons of the butter with the remaining 2 tablespoons olive oil. Add the chopped white part of the rampions and the garlic and cook until the rampions are tender and the garlic is barely browned, about 4 minutes. Add the rice and stir until the grains are coated with oil and very light golden, about 3 minutes. Pour in the wine and stir until it is just absorbed by the rice. Add enough chicken stock to cover the rice by 12 mm (½ inch), about 250 ml (8 fl oz), and stir constantly until it is absorbed. When the pan is almost dry, add another cup of chicken stock and cook, stirring constantly, until the pan is almost dry again. Continue adding stock to cover and stirring constantly, always waiting until the previous addition is absorbed, until the rice is almost al dente. The total cooking time will be about 20 minutes.

6 Stir in the asparagus, peas, and mushrooms and cook for 3 minutes. Add the reserved pine nuts and the parsley and cook for about 1 minute, just to warm through. Stir in the remaining 2 tablespoons of butter and the cheese and season to taste with salt and pepper. The risotto should be the consistency of loose porridge. If it is too thick, stir in some chicken stock. If it is too loose, add a little more cheese. Divide the risotto among shallow warmed individual bowls. Sprinkle the risotto with the rampion tops and serve at once, handing additional cheese at the table.

Serve with a soft, medium-bodied Merlot.

SAUTÉED CALF'S LIVER WITH MUSTARD-SHALLOT SAUCE

Sautéed calf's liver is classic New York fare, found in every diner and in the most elegant restaurants, such as Daniel, which is as grand as it gets. From the moment you walk through the bronze-studded doors until you receive a basket of warm madeleines, you are treated to an unparalleled dining experience. This recipe, from owner Daniel Boulud, is a classic of Lyons, his birthplace. When not overseeing his restaurants, he is a guest lecturer at the French Culinary Institute in SoHo and the Culinary Institute of America in Hyde Park.

1 Rinse the liver slices and pat dry with kitchen towels. Season on both sides with salt and pepper. In a large frying pan over high heat, warm the rapeseed oil. Pour the flour on to a plate. Dredge each liver slice in the flour, shaking off the excess. When the oil is hot, lay the slices in the pan and sear for 3–4 minutes. Carefully turn the slices and sear on the other side for 3–4 minutes. Transfer to a plate and keep warm.

2 In the same frying pan over medium heat, melt the butter. Add the shallots and cook, stirring frequently, until tender, 2–3 minutes. Add the vinegar and cook until almost evaporated, 2–3 minutes. Add the white wine and deglaze the pan, stirring to dislodge the browned bits at the bottom of the pan, 2–3 minutes. Add the beef stock and cook until almost evaporated, 4–5 minutes. Stir in the cream and simmer until reduced by half, 5–6 minutes. Stir in the mustard, parsley, and tarragon and season to taste with salt and pepper.

3 Divide the liver slices among warmed individual plates. Spoon the sauce on top, dividing it evenly, and serve at once.

Serve with a sweet red wine with bracing acidity, such as a Pinot Noir.

750 g (1½ lb) calf's liver, membrane removed and cut into 4 slices, each 12 mm (½ inch) thick

Sea salt and freshly ground pepper

2 tablespoons rapeseed oil

155 g (5 oz) plain flour

2 tablespoons unsalted butter

3 shallots, finely chopped

2 tablespoons sherry vinegar or red wine vinegar

60 ml (2 fl oz) dry white wine

60 ml (2 fl oz) salt-free beef stock

60 ml (2 fl oz) double cream

2 tablespoons Dijon mustard

2 tablespoons finely chopped fresh flat-leaf parsley

1 tablespoon finely chopped fresh tarragon

Makes 4 servings

Cooking Schools

New York City is rife with talented young chefs from local cooking schools. The French Culinary Institute has graduated such notable chefs as Wylie Dufresne of WD-50 and Bobby Flay of Mesa Grill, and includes Jacques Pépin, Daniel Boulud, and Jacques Torres on the dean roster. The Institute of Culinary Education counts Babbo pastry chef Gina Di Palma and Tasting Room co-owners Colin and Renée Alevras as alumni. Five hundred new cooks are certified each year from the New School's professional culinary program, and the famed Culinary Institute of America in Hyde Park, alma mater to culinary icons like Anthony Bourdain, Rocco DiSpirito, and Alfred Portale, sends some 1,100 students into the workforce each year.

All of these schools make use of the city and its resources – farmers' markets, local artisanal products, and influential restaurants and chefs. Internships give students hands-on experience, whether they are working with food stylists, at magazines like *Saveur* and *Gourmet,* or, most often, in restaurant kitchens – Babbo, Craft, Aureole, Jean Georges, and Gotham Bar and Grill.

BUTTERFLIED CHICKEN WITH JERUSALEM ARTICHOKE AND CELERY ROOT PURÉE

Comfort food such as macaroni and cheese and roast chicken with mashed potatoes began to take hold during the mid-1980s. Union Square Café pioneered the movement with chef Michael Romano's presentations that relied on fresh produce from the nearby Union Square farmers' market. The development was not a trend after all, as New Yorkers have an unending appetite for the country-style fare served in many restaurants, including Home in the West Village, known for roast chicken and desserts such as chocolate pudding. This recipe pairs a purée of winter vegetables with a butterflied chicken.

1 chicken, about 1.5 kg (3 lb)

1½ teaspoons peppercorns

4 cloves garlic, finely chopped

2 teaspoons *each* chopped fresh thyme, rosemary, and sage

Sea salt and freshly ground pepper

1 large carrot, peeled and coarsely chopped

1 celery stalk, coarsely chopped

1 yellow onion, cut into 8 pieces

FOR THE PURÉE

450 g (1 lb) waxy potatoes

250 g (½ lb) Jerusalem artichokes

1 celeriac, about 250 g (½ lb)

60 ml (2 fl oz) single cream

60 ml (2 fl oz) chicken stock, or as needed

2 tablespoons unsalted butter, at room temperature

Sea salt and freshly ground pepper

60 ml (2 fl oz) dry red wine

250 ml (8 fl oz) chicken stock

1 tablespoon unsalted butter

Makes 4 servings

1 Preheat the grill. If the giblets and neck are in the chicken cavity, remove them and reserve for another use or discard. Remove and discard any excess fat from the cavity. To butterfly the chicken, place the bird breast side down on a cutting board. Using poultry scissors, cut down one side of the backbone, then cut down the other side of the backbone, remove it, and reserve for another use or discard. Turn the bird breast side up and spread it open as flat as possible. Using both hands, press firmly to break the breastbone and flatten the bird. Rinse the chicken and pat dry with kitchen towels.

2 With the chicken breast side up, and starting at the neck end, slip your fingers under the skin and gently separate the skin from the breast meat on both sides, being careful not to tear the skin. Then, at the opposite end, gently separate the skin from the thigh and drumstick meat. Using a mortar and pestle, coarsely grind the peppercorns. Add the garlic, herbs, and ½ teaspoon salt and grind into a paste. Reserve 2 tablespoons of the herb mixture. Place the remainder evenly under the chicken skin.

3 Place the carrot, celery, and onion pieces in a roasting pan large enough to hold the chicken. Arrange the chicken on top of the vegetables. Grill 20 cm (8 inches) from the heat source until the chicken is brown and the juices run clear when a thigh is pierced with a sharp knife, about 30 minutes.

4 Meanwhile, make the purée: Peel the potatoes, Jerusalem artichokes, and celeriac and cut into 2.5-cm (1-inch) pieces. Bring a saucepan three-quarters full of water to the boil. Add the vegetables, return to the boil, then reduce the heat to medium and simmer until very tender, about 20 minutes. Meanwhile, in a small saucepan over medium heat, warm the cream and 60 ml (2 fl oz) of the chicken stock. Drain the vegetables and pass through a ricer into a bowl. Using a wooden spoon, beat the butter into the purée, then stir in the warm cream mixture. Add more stock if the purée is too thick. Alternatively, place in a food processor, add the butter, single cream, and stock, and process to form a smooth purée. Season to taste with salt and pepper. Cover tightly with aluminium foil to keep warm before serving.

5 When the chicken is done, transfer it to a platter and tent loosely with aluminium foil. Spoon off the fat from the roasting pan. Place the pan over medium-high heat, add the red wine and chicken stock, bring to the boil and deglaze the pan, stirring to scrape up any browned bits. Add the reserved herb mixture and cook until the liquid is reduced by half, 4–5 minutes. Remove from the heat and whisk in the butter. Strain the sauce, discarding the vegetables, and season to taste with salt and pepper.

6 To serve, use kitchen scissors to cut along the breastbone and split the chicken in half. Cut the chicken into quarters or remove the legs and wings and slice the meat from the breast. Divide the purée evenly among warmed individual plates. Divide the chicken among the plates and top with the sauce. Serve at once.

Serve with a creamy, oaky Chardonnay.

HERB-CRUSTED RACK OF LAMB WITH SHELL BEAN RAGOUT

The best New York chefs are devoted to sourcing the finest-quality meat, poultry, fish, fruit, and vegetables from small regional farmers. Bill Telepan, chef-owner of the former Judson Grill in Midtown, is known for his exclusive use of meat from small farms. For this dish, he buys lamb from Jamison Farm in Pennsylvania. Fed on herbs and native grasses, such as bluegrass and wild clover, and slaughtered at a young age, Jamison lamb is regarded as among the most flavoursome in the country. Fresh beans, served with the lamb, have a creamy, tender quality and are coveted during their short season in late summer.

1 To prepare the beans, if using dried beans, pick over them, discarding any misshapen ones or grit. Rinse the beans well, put them in a bowl and add water to cover by about 7.5 cm (3 inches). Let soak for at least 4 hours or up to overnight. (Alternatively, for a quick soak, bring the beans and water to a rapid simmer and cook for 2 minutes. Remove from the heat, cover and let stand for 1 hour.) Drain the beans and set aside.

2 In a large saucepan over medium heat, warm the olive oil. Add the onion and chopped garlic, cover and cook, stirring occasionally, until the onion is tender, about 7 minutes. Add the fresh beans or drained, soaked beans and the stock. Bring to a simmer over medium heat and cook until the beans are tender, 15–20 minutes for fresh beans, 45–90 minutes for dried beans, depending on the variety used. If using dried beans, check the liquid every 30 minutes and add water if the beans become exposed. Using a mortar and pestle, mash the whole garlic clove into a paste. Transfer to a small bowl, add the butter, vinegar, ½ teaspoon salt, and ¼ teaspoon pepper, and mix with a fork until blended. Swirl into the warm beans. Taste and adjust the seasoning with salt and pepper.

3 Meanwhile, to prepare the lamb, preheat the oven to 230°C (450°F). To french the bones, trim most of the fat from each rack. Insert the blade of a sharp knife into the meat and tissue on each side of the bones to mark what should be cut away. Use the knife and your fingers to cut and pull out the meat and tissue from between the bones, working up to 5 cm (2 inches) from the ends of the bones. Using the back of the knife blade, scrape off any remaining meat or tissue to leave the bones nearly clean.

4 In a large roasting tin or cast-iron frying pan, over medium-high heat, warm the olive oil. Lay the racks meat side down in the pan and sear to a rich brown colour, 4–5 minutes. Transfer the pan to the oven and roast for 7 minutes. Remove from the oven, turn the lamb over and roast for 5–7 minutes for medium-rare, 8–10 minutes for medium. Remove from the oven, tent with aluminium foil, and let the meat rest for 15 minutes.

5 While the lamb is resting, in a sauté pan over high heat, melt the butter (but do not brown). Add the breadcrumbs and sauté until lightly toasted, 3–5 minutes. Transfer to a bowl. Stir in the parsley, marjoram, and thyme and season with salt and pepper to taste. If necessary, reheat the beans over medium heat, stirring occasionally.

6 Brush the lamb with olive oil and sprinkle with the breadcrumb mixture, pressing it into the meat to make it adhere. Cut each rack into chops. Divide the beans among warmed individual plates and arrange 2 chops on each plate on top of the beans. Serve at once.

Serve with a rich Merlot.

FOR THE BEANS

315 g (10 oz) shelled fresh beans, such as borlotti, flageolet, runner, or cannellini beans or 140 g (4½ oz) dried beans

1 tablespoon olive oil

½ small yellow onion, finely chopped

2 cloves garlic, 1 finely chopped and 1 left whole

1 l (1¾ pints) chicken stock, vegetable stock, or water

60 g (2 oz) unsalted butter, at room temperature

1 tablespoon red wine vinegar

Sea salt and freshly ground pepper

FOR THE LAMB

2 racks of lamb, 8 ribs and 750 g–1 kg (1½–2¼ lb) each

60 ml (2 fl oz) olive oil, plus more for brushing

2 tablespoons unsalted butter

30 g (1 oz) dried breadcrumbs

1 tablespoon chopped fresh flat-leaf parsley

1 teaspoon *each* chopped fresh marjoram and thyme

Makes 4 servings

SOFT-SHELLED CRABS WITH ROMESCO SAUCE

Every year in the late spring, Union Square Café's loyal customers look forward to the arrival of the first soft-shelled crabs — young blue crabs that are harvested in waters along the eastern seaboard from New Jersey to South Carolina, the most famous of which are from Maryland. Chef Michael Romano's pioneering food and owner Danny Meyer's impeccable service standards have earned the café the honour of "New York's Favourite Restaurant" in the Zagat Survey *since 1997. Romano serves the crabs with his own creamy version of* romesco *sauce, and pairs them with a green salad tossed with seasonal vegetables.*

FOR THE SAUCE

60 g (2 oz) whole almonds

250 g (8 oz) mayonnaise

375 g (¾ lb) tomatoes, peeled, seeded and finely chopped

1 tablespoon tomato purée

60 ml (2 fl oz) red wine vinegar, or to taste

2 tablespoons chopped fresh flat-leaf parsley

2 cloves garlic, finely chopped

Pinch of cayenne pepper, or to taste

Sea salt and freshly ground black pepper

FOR THE CRABS

8 soft-shelled crabs, each about 75–90 g (2½–3 oz)

60 g (2 oz) plain flour

Sea salt and freshly ground black pepper

80 ml (3 fl oz) olive oil

Makes 4 servings

1 To make the sauce, preheat the oven to 180°C (350°F). Spread the almonds on a baking sheet and toast until lightly browned, about 10 minutes. Pour onto a plate, let cool and then coarsely chop. In a non-reactive bowl, combine the toasted almonds, mayonnaise, tomatoes, tomato purée, ¼ cup vinegar, parsley, garlic, and a pinch of cayenne pepper, and stir well to combine. Season to taste with salt and black pepper. Taste and adjust the seasoning with vinegar and/or cayenne pepper. Cover and refrigerate until ready to use.

2 Reduce the oven temperature to 120°C (250°F). To clean the crabs, briefly rinse each crab under cold running water. Pull off and discard the apron, the small triangular flap of shell on the underside. Using a small knife, remove the eyes by making a small cut behind the mouth and eyes; be careful not to remove the entire head. Gently squeeze the body and use the point of the knife to pull out the small sac behind the mouth. Fold back the points of the top shell on either side of the crab and pull out the spongy, feather-shaped white gills (dead man's fingers) and discard.

3 On a large plate, combine the flour, ½ teaspoon salt, and ⅛ teaspoon black pepper. Dredge each crab in the seasoned flour, shaking off the excess. Set aside on a plate.

4 In a large frying pan over medium-high heat, heat the olive oil just until it begins to smoke. Lay 4 of the crabs, shell side down, in the pan and cook until reddish brown, 3–4 minutes. Using tongs, turn the crabs and cook until reddish brown on the other side, 3–4 minutes. Transfer to an ovenproof plate lined with kitchen towels and place in the oven to keep warm while cooking the remaining crabs.

5 Divide the crabs among warmed individual plates. Serve at once with the *romesco* sauce for dipping.

Serve with a crisp, acidic Pinot Grigio.

SKATE WITH MUSTARD BUTTER

Skate is a saltwater fish shaped like a kite, harvested in the Atlantic and the Pacific. Its fins, often called wings, are the edible portions and have a sweet, scallop-like flavour. Even though skate has long been enjoyed in Europe, only in recent years has it been found on the menus of some of New York's finest, most creative restaurants, such as Le Bernardin, WD-50, and The Harrison. This version has been a staple at Blue Ribbon's flagship restaurant in SoHo since chef-owners Bruce and Eric Bromberg opened it in the early 1990s.

1 Preheat the oven to 140°C (275°F). Place the bread cubes on a baking sheet. Drizzle with the olive oil, toss to coat and spread out evenly. Bake until golden and crisp, stirring occasionally, 7–8 minutes.

2 In a large frying pan over medium-high heat, fry the bacon, stirring occasionally until it begins to turn crisp, about 5 minutes. Add the potatoes and cook, stirring occasionally, until light golden and tender, about 8 minutes. Add the prawns and parsley and cook, stirring occasionally, just until the prawns turn pink, about 3 minutes. Season to taste with salt and pepper. Set aside.

3 In a small frying pan over medium heat, melt 4 tablespoons of the butter and cook until light brown, about 3 minutes. Whisk in the mustard and cook, whisking constantly, just until the mustard is warmed through.

4 Pour the flour on a plate. In a non-stick frying pan over medium heat, melt the remaining 2 tablespoons butter. Rinse the skate fillets and pat dry with kitchen towels. Season both sides with salt and pepper. Dredge each fillet in the flour, shaking off the excess. Lay the fillets in the pan and cook until lightly browned, about 3 minutes. Turn and cook until opaque throughout and browned on the second side, about 3 minutes.

5 Divide the bacon mixture among warmed individual plates. Top with a skate fillet and drizzle with some of the mustard butter. Sprinkle the toasted bread cubes on top and serve at once.

Serve with a fruity, oaky Chardonnay.

2 slices good white bread, cut into 6-mm (¼-inch) cubes, (about 60 g [2 oz])

1 tablespoon olive oil

90 g (3 oz) salted pork belly or slab bacon, finely diced

2 round red or white potatoes, boiled until tender, peeled, and very finely diced

16 large raw prawns, peeled, deveined, and sliced horizontally into 3 pieces

15 g (½ oz) fresh flat-leaf parsley leaves

Sea salt and freshly ground pepper

90 g (3 oz) unsalted butter

2½ tablespoons Dijon mustard

155 g (5 oz) plain flour

4 skate fillets, about 1.5 kg (3 lb) total weight

Makes 4 servings

Late-Night Dining

New York is as lively at night as it is during the day. With appetites kindled, New Yorkers wander out of art show openings, theatres and clubs expecting a full buffet of options, from ethnic cafés to fine restaurants, to welcome them with open doors and full menus. In Greenwich Village, patrons line up until the early-morning hours at Joe's Pizza for slices. New Yorkers also know they can head for all-nighters such as Florent, a fixture in the Meatpacking District that serves hearty bistro fare at all hours except one (5 A.M. to 6 A.M.). Across town, in the East Village, Ukrainian diner Veselka ladles out its famous borscht to a crowd of New York University students and neighbourhood regulars twenty-four hours a day, every day of the year.

The *grande dame* of late-night dining is Blue Ribbon in SoHo, known as a hangout for restaurant employees, including many big-name chefs, just off work. Bruce and Eric Bromberg's menu offers a familiar, if eclectic, selection of starters and main courses, including matzo ball soup, oysters, and fried chicken. It's not unusual to walk in well after midnight and find there's an hour-long wait!

BAKED ZITI WITH SAUSAGE, EGGPLANT, AND PEAS

Baked ziti is part of New York's Italian American culture. It is a culinary descendant of the "old country", Sicily, where ziti as long as spaghetti is broken up into small pieces to make timballos. *Families might serve these baked pastas for a Sunday lunch or other special occasion. Sometimes called "pasta Siciliano", baked ziti is on the menu of about every restaurant in the Arthur Avenue section of the Bronx. Some cooks use fresh mozzarella cheese; others add a layer of ricotta in the centre. This hearty version uses mozzarella and Parmesan, as well as a trio of meats.*

1 large aubergine, cut into 12-mm (½-inch) cubes

Sea salt and freshly ground pepper

60 ml (2 fl oz) olive oil, plus more for frying

1 yellow onion, diced

1 celery stalk, diced

1 carrot, peeled and diced

4 cloves garlic, finely chopped

250 g (½ lb) sweet Italian pork sausage, casings removed and crumbled

250 g (½ lb) minced veal

250 g (½ lb) minced beef

250 ml (8 fl oz) dry red wine

2 tablespoons tomato purée

750 ml (1¼ pints) tomato passata

2 tablespoons sugar

185 g (6 oz) frozen petits pois

450 g (1 lb) ziti

250 g (½ lb) fresh mozzarella, cut into 6-mm (¼-inch) cubes

125 g (¼ lb) freshly grated Parmesan, plus more for serving

Makes 8 servings

1 Place the cubed aubergine in a colander over a plate. Sprinkle generously with salt, toss to coat, and let stand for 30 minutes to drain. Rinse the aubergine under cold water and pat dry with kitchen towels.

2 In a large pot over medium heat, warm the olive oil. Add the onion and sauté until translucent, about 5 minutes. Add the celery and carrot and sauté until tender, about 10 minutes longer. Add the garlic and cook until fragrant, about 2 minutes. Add the crumbled sausage meat and minced veal and beef and cook, stirring and breaking up the meat, until lightly browned, about 5 minutes. Stir in the red wine and cook off the alcohol, 3–4 minutes. Stir in the tomato purée and season with salt and pepper. Add the tomato passata and sugar, reduce the heat to low and cook until the sauce thickens, about 30 minutes.

3 Meanwhile, in a large frying pan over medium-high heat, pour in the olive oil to reach a depth of 2.5 cm (1 inch). When the oil is very hot and almost smoking, working in batches to avoid crowding, add a single layer of aubergine cubes and fry, turning once or twice, until golden on all sides, 8–10 minutes. Using a slotted spoon, transfer to kitchen towels to drain.

4 Reserve 250 ml (8 fl oz) of the sauce. Stir the petits pois and fried aubergine into the remaining sauce and simmer over medium heat until the petits pois are just tender, 5–10 minutes. Keep warm.

5 Preheat the oven to 190°C (375°F). Lightly oil a 23-x-33-cm (9-x-13-inch) baking dish or 8 individual baking dishes.

6 Bring a large pot of water to the boil. Generously salt the boiling water, add the ziti and cook until al dente, 10–12 minutes. Drain the ziti, reserving 500 ml (16 fl oz) of the pasta water. Transfer the ziti to the pot with the sauce. Add 125 ml (4 fl oz) of the pasta water and toss. Add more pasta water if the pasta is sticky. Add two-thirds of the mozzarella and quickly toss again. Pour the ziti into the prepared baking dish or divide among the individual dishes. Press the pasta down with your hands. Scatter the remaining mozzarella cubes over the top and sprinkle with the Parmesan, dividing the cheeses evenly if using individual dishes.

7 Bake until the cheese is melted and the top is light golden, about 25 minutes for the large dish or 20 minutes for the individual dishes. Remove from the oven and let rest for 5 minutes before serving. If necessary, warm the reserved sauce over medium heat. Spoon some of the reserved sauce over each serving and pass the grated Parmesan at the table.

Serve with a peppery, spicy red wine such as a Syrah.

BURGERS WITH ONION JAM

New York burger zealots have long debated the merits of favourites, from patty melts to fancy hamburgers carrying a steak dinner price. The first expensive version to gain notoriety was the "21 Burger", sold for $21 during the 1980s at the famous "21" Club in Midtown. The burger was soon eclipsed when Old Homestead Steak House began selling a $41 burger made with Japanese Kobe beef. In 2001, Daniel Boulud's DB Bistro Moderne won the much-publicised "burger war" with the DB Burger Royale — an extravagant ground sirloin hamburger stuffed with foie gras, braised short ribs and black truffles.

1 To make the onion jam, in a large sauté pan over medium heat, melt the butter with the olive oil. Add the sweet onions and cook, stirring occasionally and reducing the heat if they begin to brown, until they are tender and translucent, 10–15 minutes. Stir in the cider vinegar and balsamic vinegar, brown sugar, 1 teaspoon salt, ½ teaspoon pepper, and 60 ml (2 fl oz) water. Reduce the heat to low and simmer until the onion mixture has a jamlike consistency, 15–20 minutes. Add more water if the onions are sticking to the pan. Taste and adjust the seasoning with salt and pepper. Set aside.

2 To make the burgers, prepare a charcoal or gas barbecue for direct grilling over high heat or preheat the grill. In a bowl, combine the minced beef, egg yolks, spring onions, 1 teaspoon salt, and ¼ teaspoon pepper. Dampen your hands and mix the ingredients until well blended, then shape into 4 round patties,

each 2.5 cm (1 inch) thick. Place on the barbecue rack or under the grill, and cook, turning once, for 4 minutes per side for medium-rare, 4½ minutes per side for medium, or 5 minutes per side for well-done.

3 While the burgers are grilling, in a small bowl, stir together the mayonnaise and horseradish sauce. Spread the mixture on 4 slices of the toasted bread. Spread the Dijon mustard on the remaining slices, and then spread with the pâté, if using.

4 Place a burger on each Dijon-covered bread slice. Top each with some of the onion jam and bread-and-butter pickles, a lettuce leaf, and a mayonnaise-covered bread slice. Serve at once.

Serve with a medium-bodied red such as a blend of Cabernet Sauvignon and Cabernet Franc.

FOR THE ONION JAM

2 tablespoons unsalted butter

2 tablespoons olive oil

2 sweet onions, halved and thinly sliced

60 ml (2 fl oz) *each* cider vinegar and balsamic vinegar

105 g (3½ oz) firmly packed golden brown sugar

Sea salt and freshly ground pepper

FOR THE BURGERS

750 g (1½ lb) minced beef chuck

2 egg yolks

3 spring onions, white parts only, finely chopped

Sea salt and freshly ground pepper

3 tablespoons mayonnaise

2 tablespoons horseradish sauce

8 slices crusty Italian bread, each 12 mm (½ inch) thick, toasted

Dijon mustard

125 g (¼ lb) smooth duck or goose pâté (optional)

Bread-and-butter pickles* or other pickles

4 Bibb lettuce leaves

Makes 4 servings

*Bread-and-butter pickles are made from pickling thin slices of unpeeled cucumber in a brine containing onion, mustard, celery seeds, cloves, and turmeric and sweetened with sugar.

MISO-MARINATED BLACK COD

When Nobu Restaurant opened in Tribeca in 1995, New Yorkers flocked to it for many reasons – including its much-touted chef, Nobu Matsuhisa; its celebrity partner, Tribeca resident Robert DeNiro; and New York's legendary restaurateur, Drew Nieporent. But it was the black cod that diners talked about. The lone fillet arrived on a plate with just the caramelised exterior set against the glistening snow-white flesh underneath. It was astonishing that something so simple could have so much flavour. A similar dish has become a staple at Japanese and fusion restaurants all over town.

125 ml (4 fl oz) mirin

80 ml (3 fl oz) sake

250 ml (8 fl oz) white miso

125 g (4 oz) sugar

4 black cod fillets*, about 185 g (6 oz) each

Makes 4 servings

1 In a saucepan over medium heat, combine the mirin and sake and simmer to evaporate the alcohol, about 1 minute. Add the miso and sugar and stir with a wooden spoon until smooth. Bring to a simmer and cook, stirring constantly, until the sugar dissolves, about 3 minutes. Set aside to cool.

2 Rinse the black cod fillets and pat dry with kitchen towels. Reserve 3 tablespoons of the marinade in an airtight container in the refrigerator for later use. Pour half of the remaining miso marinade into a shallow non-reactive dish large enough to hold the fillets in a single layer. Add the fillets and pour the remaining marinade over the fish. Cover and refrigerate for at least 2 days or up to 3 days. Bring the fish and the reserved marinade to room temperature before using.

3 Preheat the grill. Remove the black cod fillets from the marinade and lightly wipe off any excess with kitchen towels. Discard the marinade. Arrange the fillets in a single layer, without touching, on a baking sheet. Grill them 20 cm (8 inches) from the heat source until the fish is caramelised and a rich brown colour, about 10 minutes. Remove from the oven, turn the fillets and grill them just until the flesh flakes easily, 3–5 minutes longer.

4 Divide the fillets among warmed individual plates. Drizzle with the reserved marinade and serve.

Serve with a rich, smooth, spicy Viognier such as Casa Larga Viognier from the Finger Lakes or an Australian Shiraz.

*Black or smallscale cod (*Notothenia microlepidota*) is found in Atlantic waters and is not related to the true cod. Cod, hake, haddock, or similar firm-fleshed white fish can be substituted if it is not available.

SIDE DISHES

Vegetables for side dishes may come from the Hudson River Valley

or Long Island, but they are flavoured with seasonings from other continents.

New Yorkers are known to wax romantic about the region's four distinct seasons, and nowhere is this sentiment more apparent than in the side dishes on both restaurant menus and home tables. A main dish might remain the same year-round, but the availability of vegetables marks seasonal rhythms: Swiss chard in spring, sweetcorn in summer, Brussels sprouts in autumn, and root vegetables in winter. Preparations take advantage of New York's global palate. Cauliflower is given a Sicilian inflection with capers and raisins, a gratin of potatoes and fennel has a French accent, and broccoli rabe with roasted garlic evokes northern Italy.

POTATO, FENNEL, AND THREE-CHEESE GRATIN

New York's contemporary food scene can trace its origins to the French cuisine served at Le Pavillion, arguably the most influential restaurant in New York City's history. Le Pavillion and the restaurants it spawned are now closed, but a new generation of French restaurants, brasseries and bistros proves that New Yorkers are as loyal to French food as ever. Many still visit institutions like Daniel, Le Bernardin, Chanterelle, and Jean Georges. Others prefer such French bistros as Raoul's, Les Halles, Quatorze Bis, Balthazar, and Pastis. This simple gratin is a typical New York twist on a classic bistro side dish.

1 Preheat the oven to 180°C (350°F). In a heavy-bottomed saucepan, combine the cream, stock, butter, garlic, bay leaf, thyme sprigs, dried chilli flakes, nutmeg, 2 teaspoons salt, and ½ teaspoon black pepper. Bring to the boil over medium heat, reduce the heat to low and simmer gently to infuse the cream with the seasoning, about 15 minutes.

2 Meanwhile, using a mandoline or a sharp knife, slice the potatoes paper-thin. Cut off the stems and feathery leaves from each fennel bulb and discard. Discard the outer layer of the bulb if it is tough, and cut away any discoloured areas. Quarter the bulb lengthways and cut away any tough base portions. Cut the quarters lengthways into thin strips, about 6 mm (¼ inch) wide.

3 In a small bowl, stir together the Parmesan, Gruyère and Fontina cheeses. Arrange one-quarter of the potato slices in the bottom of a 10-x-30-cm (8-x-12-inch) gratin or shallow 2 l (3½ pint) baking dish. Sprinkle evenly with 30 g (1 oz) of the cheese mixture. Top with one-third of the fennel strips, distributing them evenly, then sprinkle with another 30 g (1 oz) of the cheese mixture. Repeat the layers – you should have a total of four layers of potato slices and three layers of fennel strips, ending with a layer of potato slices. Pour the cream mixture through a medium-mesh sieve over the top. Sprinkle evenly with the remaining 60 g (2 oz) of the cheese mixture.

4 Cover the baking dish tightly with aluminium foil. Bake for 1 hour. Remove and discard the foil and continue to bake the gratin until the potatoes are tender and the gratin is golden brown and bubbling, about 30 minutes longer. Remove from the oven and let the gratin stand 10–15 minutes before serving.

250 ml (8 fl oz) double cream

430 ml (14 fl oz) chicken stock

3 tablespoons unsalted butter

2 cloves garlic, crushed

1 bay leaf

2 sprigs fresh thyme

Pinch of dried chilli flakes

Pinch of freshly grated nutmeg

Sea salt and freshly ground black pepper

1 kg (2¼ lb) waxy potatoes, peeled

2 fennel bulbs, about 450 g (1 lb) total weight

60 g (2 oz) freshly grated Parmesan cheese

90 g (3 oz) coarsely grated Gruyère cheese

90 g (3 oz) coarsely grated Fontina cheese

Makes 8 servings

CREAMED SWISS CHARD

Much of New York cuisine consists of taking the classics and revising them, but only slightly. Chard, a more hearty alternative to leafy greens such as spinach, can be roasted, braised or, as here, used as a variation on creamed spinach, a ubiquitous à la carte option at traditional New York steak houses. At Del Frisco's Double Eagle Steak House, a favourite of former mayor Rudolph Giuliani, chard is sautéed with shallots and garlic. Just enough cream is added to this version to soften the flavour and texture of the somewhat bitter greens. They make a wonderful accompaniment to duck, chicken, lamb, and steak.

1.8 kg (4 lb) Swiss chard

60 g (2 oz) unsalted butter

2 cloves garlic, crushed

1 shallot, finely chopped

60 ml (2 fl oz) double cream

Sea salt and freshly ground pepper

Makes 4 servings

1 Cut the centre ribs and stalks from the leaves and discard. Place the leaves in a large pot with 250 ml (8 fl oz) water, cover and bring to the boil over high heat. Reduce the heat to medium and cook the chard until tender, 5–7 minutes. Drain well. Transfer to a cutting board and roughly chop the chard.

2 In the same pot over medium heat, melt the butter. Add the garlic and shallot and sauté until soft, about 2 minutes. Add the chard and the cream and bring to a simmer over medium heat. Reduce the heat to low and simmer until the chard absorbs the cream, about 5 minutes. Season to taste with salt and pepper. Serve at once.

MAPLE-CARAMELIZED ROOT VEGETABLES

New York State is the fourth largest producer of maple syrup worldwide. The syrup and maple sugar candies are sold at farmers' markets around New York City during the winter. Chefs take advantage of the local commodity to sweeten and flavour an array of preparations, from marinades to ice cream. Alex Paffenroth of Paffenroth Farm, located north of New York City, is known for his wide variety of root vegetables, including such oddities as blue potatoes, white beetroot, black radishes, and white, purple and globular carrots.

1 Preheat the oven to 200°C (400°F). Peel the root vegetables. Cut long, slender vegetables such as carrots and parsnips on the diagonal into 5-cm (2-inch) pieces. Cut the turnips and other round vegetables into 5-cm (2-inch) chunks. Place on a rimmed baking sheet. Drizzle with the olive oil and maple syrup, sprinkle with salt and pepper and toss to coat with the seasoning. Spread the vegetables out in a single layer and scatter the butter pieces on top.

2 Roast the vegetables, turning them occasionally, until tender and golden brown, about 30 minutes. Transfer to a warmed serving bowl and serve at once.

750 g (1½ lb) mixed root vegetables such as carrots, parsnips, turnips, swedes, sweet potatoes, and/or salsify

60 ml (2 fl oz) extra-virgin olive oil

60 ml (2 fl oz) maple syrup

Sea salt and freshly ground pepper

2 tablespoons unsalted butter, cut into small pieces

Makes 4 servings

Hudson River Valley Farms

The Hudson River Valley has long been prized for its dramatic beauty and its rich resources, from both land and water, that feed New York City. In the 1600s, the fertile land attracted industrious immigrant farmers. These farms thrived until the arrival of commercial farming, which made it difficult for small farmers to compete in the market. Between 1996 and 2001, Dutchess County, one of the valley's five counties, lost nearly half its apple orchards to development.

As chefs became passionate about using local products and consumers grew concerned about how their food was grown, New Yorkers increasingly sought out the Hudson River Valley's bounty. Farmers gained market savvy, which helped ensure their survival. Ronnybrook Farm Dairy, for instance, changed its operation to produce milk in glass bottles. On trips to farmers' markets, growers learned the tastes of their customers and began to diversify by growing unusual varieties such as white carrots, black kale, and micro-greens. Other farmers banded together into groups or co-ops that sell their produce to some of New York's best restaurants.

ZUCCHINI WITH TOASTED ALMONDS AND PECORINO ROMANO

New York chefs travel the world looking for inspiration, which they bring home and add to their global culinary vocabulary. Jimmy Bradley, chef/co-owner of The Red Cat, The Harrison, and The Mermaid Inn, grew up in an Italian-American family whose life centred around cooking and eating. The inspiration for this recipe came from a similar dish that he discovered in a little restaurant called Rosanna e Mateo in the Jewish ghetto in Rome. This dish can be served either as a first course or as a side dish for an Italian-inspired summer meal, such as grilled steaks drizzled with olive oil.

6 medium courgettes, about 700 g (1½ lb) total weight

60 ml (2 fl oz) extra-virgin olive oil

30 g (1 oz) flaked almonds

Sea salt and freshly ground pepper

Wedge of pecorino romano cheese

Makes 4 servings

1 Trim the ends from each courgette and then cut them lengthways into slices 3 mm (⅛ inch) thick. Cut each slice into matchsticks about 3 mm (⅛ inch) wide and 5 cm (2 inches) long.

2 Divide the olive oil between 2 frying pans and place over high heat. When the oil is hot, add the almonds, dividing them between the pans, and cook, stirring constantly, until golden brown, about 2 minutes. Divide the courgettes between the pans, turn off the heat, and toss to coat with the hot oil until the they are warmed through, about 30 seconds. Season to taste with salt and pepper.

3 Divide the courgettes among warmed individual plates or mound on a warmed small serving platter. Using a vegetable peeler or a cheese plane, cut shavings from the pecorino romano wedge over the courgettes. Serve at once.

BROCCOLI RABE WITH ROASTED GARLIC

Large florets of broccoli fried in copious amounts of oil and garlic are a staple at traditional Italian restaurants in Manhattan and the outer boroughs. As newer restaurants have begun to reflect a broader spectrum of Italian regional cuisine, broccoli rabe, favoured especially in northern Italy, has grown in popularity. Known also as rapini, *it has green stalks and florets, but is more closely related to cabbage and turnips. In this version, its pleasant bitterness is balanced by the nutty, almost sweet flavour of roasted garlic. Broccoli rabe is an excellent accompaniment to roasted pork, grilled steak, or pasta.*

1 To make the roasted garlic, preheat the oven to 180°C (350°F). Break the head of garlic into individual cloves. Stack 2 pieces of aluminium foil each about 15 cm (6 inches) square. Place the cloves in the centre, drizzle with the olive oil and sprinkle with salt and black pepper. Bring up the corners of the foil and fold together to make a tight packet. Roast the garlic until soft and creamy, 30–40 minutes. Let the garlic cool slightly, then when it is cool enough to touch, squeeze the garlic out of the peels. Discard the skins.

2 Meanwhile, trim off and discard the tough stem ends from the broccoli rabe. Place the broccoli rabe in a large saucepan with 125 ml (4 fl oz) water. Cover and bring the water to the boil over high heat.

Reduce the heat to medium-low and cook until tender and bright green, about 5 minutes. Drain and cut into 2.5-cm (1-inch) pieces.

3 In a large sauté pan over medium heat, warm the olive oil. Add the dried chilli flakes and the roasted garlic along with any oil in the foil packet and sauté for 3–4 minutes to flavour the oil. Add the broccoli rabe, stir to combine and sauté until heated through, about 3 minutes. Season to taste with salt and black pepper and serve.

FOR THE ROASTED GARLIC

1 head garlic

2 tablespoons extra-virgin olive oil

Sea salt and freshly ground black pepper

1.3 kg (3 lb) broccoli rabe

60 ml (2 fl oz) olive oil

Pinch of dried chilli flakes

Makes 6 servings

BRUSSELS SPROUTS WITH BACON VINAIGRETTE

In the autumn, after the first frost has hit area farms, cruciferous vegetables, including cauliflower, cabbage, broccoli, leafy greens, and brussels sprouts, replace tomatoes and sweetcorn on market-driven menus across the city. In the hands of skilled cooks, the oft-maligned Brussels sprout has a distinct, nutty flavour that comes through in simple preparations. At Mario Batali's tapas restaurant, Casa Mono, they are cooked on the grill and tossed with lemon and thyme. Brussels sprouts are also enhanced by stronger flavours such as bacon and balsamic vinegar, as in this preparation.

6 rashers bacon

2 tablespoons white balsamic vinegar or balsamic vinegar

½ teaspoon Dijon mustard

1 clove garlic, finely chopped

1 teaspoon chopped fresh thyme

125 ml (4 fl oz) extra-virgin olive oil

Sea salt and freshly ground pepper

700 g (1½ lb) Brussels sprouts

2 tablespoons unsalted butter

Makes 6 servings

1 In a frying pan over medium-low heat, fry the bacon rashers, turning occasionally, until crisp, 7–8 minutes. Transfer to kitchen towels to drain.

2 Meanwhile, in a small bowl, whisk together the vinegar, mustard, garlic, and thyme. Whisking constantly, pour in the olive oil in a slow, steady stream. Season to taste with salt and pepper.

3 Remove the outer leaves from each Brussels sprout and discard any that are blemished. Continue to remove the leaves, using a small, sharp knife to cut away the core. In a large saucepan over medium heat, melt the butter. Add the Brussels sprout leaves and 125 ml (4 fl oz) water, cover, raise the heat to high and bring to the boil. Reduce the heat to medium-low and cook the leaves until bright green and tender, about 7 minutes, adding more water to the pot if it is dry. Drain and transfer to a serving bowl.

4 Crumble the bacon and add it to the olive oil mixture. Drizzle it over the Brussels sprout leaves and toss to coat. Season to taste with salt and pepper. Transfer to a warmed serving bowl and serve at once.

LONG ISLAND SUCCOTASH SALAD

This salad is a tribute to those few weeks of the year in late summer when fresh beans are in abundance, juicy corn cobs are piled high at farm stands, and potatoes are so fresh that they cook almost instantly. In the Hamptons, it is a ritual at some farm stands to roast the corn, as is called for in this salad, which makes it slightly chewy and enhances its sweetness. This version of succotash is the kind of updated country fare found at many high-end food shops in the Hamptons, such as Loaves and Fishes, as well as in New York City.

1 Preheat the oven to 200°C (400°F). Place the sweetcorn kernels on a baking sheet. Drizzle with 2 tablespoons of the olive oil and season with salt and pepper. Toss to coat the kernels with the seasoning and spread out in an even layer. Roast until the sweetcorn is light brown and slightly shrivelled, about 15 minutes.

2 Meanwhile, bring a saucepan three-quarters full of water to the boil. Add the broad beans and blanch for 1 minute. Drain and rinse under cold running water. Pinch each bean to slip it from the skin. Set aside.

3 In a large frying pan over medium heat, combine the rest of the olive oil and 125 ml (4 fl oz) water. Add the potatoes, season with salt and pepper, cover, bring to a simmer and cook until the potatoes are tender and begin to sizzle, 10–20 minutes. The cooking time will depend on the size and freshness of the potatoes; add more water to the pan if it is dry before the potatoes are tender. Uncover the pan, toss the potatoes in the oil remaining in the pan, and sauté until light golden, about 5 minutes.

4 To make the vinaigrette, in a small bowl, stir together the vinegar, mustard, and honey. Whisk in the olive oil and season to taste with salt and pepper.

5 In a large bowl, combine the sweetcorn, beans, potatoes, onion, parsley, and thyme. Drizzle with the vinaigrette and toss gently to coat. Serve at once.

FOR THE SALAD

6 sweetcorn cobs, kernels cut off cobs

90 ml (3 fl oz) olive oil

Sea salt and freshly ground pepper

315 g (10 oz) shelled fresh broad beans

500 g (1 lb) small new potatoes such as fingerling, Jersey royals, or red-skinned, quartered

¼ red onion, cut into paper-thin slices

2 tablespoons finely chopped fresh flat-leaf parsley

2 teaspoons chopped fresh thyme

FOR THE VINAIGRETTE

3 tablespoons red wine vinegar

½ teaspoon Dijon mustard

1 teaspoon honey

80 ml (3 fl oz) extra-virgin olive oil

Sea salt and freshly ground pepper

Makes 6–8 servings

Long Island Wineries

The east end of Long Island is most famously known for the Hamptons, the playground of the expendable-income crowd. Yet the area is gaining another image as one of the most promising new wine regions. Alex and Louisa Hargrave, founders of Hargrave Vineyards, were pioneers in 1975 when they planted the first vineyard on what had been maize and potato fields in the North Fork town of Cutchogue. The well-drained, sandy soil and the maritime climate proved ideal for creating well-balanced, fruity wines with lively acidity. Thirty years later, Long Island, primarily the North Fork, has more than three thousand acres of wine grapes and thirty wineries producing nationally recognised Merlots, Cabernet Sauvignons, and Chardonnays.

These are the kinds of wines that David Page and Barbara Shinn, owners of Home, a restaurant in Greenwich Village, and Shinn Vineyards on the North Fork, believe taste great with food. Home's wine list contains only East Coast wines. At Vintage New York, a SoHo wine store devoted exclusively to New York State wines, all of the two hundred varieties carried can be sampled by the glass.

ROASTED CAULIFLOWER, SICILIAN STYLE

Three centuries ago, long before Southampton became the fashionable home of enormous estates and million-dollar cottages, it was a farming community where potatoes, strawberries, and cauliflower were the main crops. Today, New York State still ranks third among the nation's cauliflower producers, though the primary growing areas have shifted to the Hudson River Valley and further upstate. In the autumn and winter, New York cooks use cauliflower in many ways. From soups to curries, served plain or roasted, the versatile vegetable is found in restaurants throughout the city.

2 tablespoons capers, preferably salt packed

1 head cauliflower, about 450 g (1 lb), cored and cut into florets about 2.5 cm (1 inch) in diameter

90 g (3 oz) sultanas

60 ml (2 fl oz) extra-virgin olive oil

Sea salt and freshly ground pepper

2 tablespoons finely chopped fresh flat-leaf parsley

Makes 4 servings

1 Preheat the oven to 200°C (400°F). If using salt-packed capers, rinse and pat dry with a kitchen towel. Combine the cauliflower florets, sultanas and capers on a rimmed baking sheet. Drizzle with the olive oil, sprinkle with salt and pepper and toss to coat. Spread the florets out in an even layer.

2 Roast the cauliflower, stirring occasionally, until golden brown, 20–25 minutes. Transfer to a warmed serving bowl. Sprinkle with 1 tablespoon of the parsley and toss to combine. Sprinkle the remaining parsley over the top. Serve warm or at room temperature.

DESSERTS

Seasonal fruits are enjoyed in crumbles, tarts, sorbets, and ice creams, but for many

New Yorkers there is no better finish to a meal than a thick slice of cheesecake.

Many a dessert begins with fruit. Summer's blueberries are turned into sorbet and ice cream, served with golden sugar biscuits. A classic crumble pairs sweet strawberries and tart rhubarb and is embellished with a scoop of tangy buttermilk ice cream. Autumn is the time to make a rustic tart using the apples harvested north of the city. At even the finest restaurants, diners like to end a meal with a country-style bread pudding or an updated French speciality like profiteroles. Customers line up at bakeries to purchase decorated cupcakes or at delis to order a thick slice of the city's most beloved and iconic dessert – New York cheesecake.

NEW YORK CHEESECAKE

Cheesecake is found on the menus of every New York diner and some upscale restaurants like Daniel and Gramercy Tavern. The debate about which is the best, however, is limited to a few cakes that define the genre, such as Lindy's citrus-laced cheesecake and Veniero's Sicilian-style ricotta cake, made by the bakery for more than a century. Junior's, the venerated house of cheesecake on Flatbush Avenue, uses a thin layer of sponge cake as a base. Here, a fluffy Junior's-style filling is paired with a digestive biscuit crumb crust.

1 To make the crust, preheat the oven to 180°C (325°F). Generously butter the bottom and sides of a 23-cm (9-inch) springform tin. In a bowl, combine the melted butter, digestive biscuit crumbs, and sugar and stir until the crumbs are evenly moistened. Transfer the crumb mixture to the prepared springform tin and press evenly on to the bottom and about 4 cm (1½ inches) up the sides. Bake until the crust dries out slightly, about 10 minutes. Transfer to a wire rack and let cool completely.

2 To make the filling, place the cream cheese in a large bowl. Using an electric mixer on high speed, beat until smooth, about 5 minutes. In a bowl, mix together the sugar and flour. Add to the cream cheese and beat until well blended, stopping frequently to scrape down the sides of the bowl with a rubber spatula. Add the eggs and egg yolk, one at a time, beating after each addition and again stopping to scrape down the sides of the bowl. Add the cream and vanilla and beat until combined. Pour the cream cheese mixture into the prepared crust.

3 Bake until the cheesecake is set and the centre jiggles slightly, 80–90 minutes (be careful not to over-bake). Transfer the cheesecake to a rack and let cool in the pan. Cover with clingfilm and refrigerate for at least 4 hours or up to overnight.

4 Unclasp the pan sides and remove. To cut the cheesecake, run a thin-bladed knife under hot running water and wipe dry before each cut. Cut the cake into wedges and serve chilled.

FOR THE CRUST

75 g (2½ oz) unsalted butter, melted, plus more for greasing the tin

112 g (3¾ oz) digestive biscuit crumbs

2 tablespoons sugar

FOR THE FILLING

1.2 kg (2½ lb) cream cheese, at warm room temperature

450 g (1 lb) sugar

60 g (2 oz) plain flour

2 medium eggs, plus 1 medium egg yolk

250 ml (8 fl oz) double cream

1 teaspoon pure vanilla extract

Makes 8–10 servings

Cheesecake

The many variations on classic cheesecake range from the cherry-topped fruit "slicks" at Carnegie Deli to cappuccino cheesecake at Eileen's, to goat's cheese and seasonal fruit versions. But simple, old-fashioned New York cheesecake with its silky, tangy flavour outshines them all.

New Yorkers willingly admit they weren't the first to create cakes based on soft, fresh cheese. European cooks had been making cheesecake in various forms for hundreds of years. But New York cheesecake, a very specific cake, owes its evolution to the arrival of cream cheese. In the late 1800s, the Empire Cheese Company in New York began producing a soft, smooth fresh cheese and named it Philadelphia. Soon afterwards, Joseph and Isaac Breakstone opened a dairy on the Lower East Side. In the 1920s, they started selling Downsville Cream Cheese.

Introduced to this new cheese, Jewish bakers made the silken-textured cake that remains a staple at Jewish delis, Greek diners, New York steakhouses, and neighbourhood bakeries throughout the five boroughs.

HONEY-POACHED QUINCES WITH FRESH RICOTTA AND PISTACHIOS

In autumn, when quinces start to arrive at the Locust Grove farm stand, currently one of the few farms at New York farmers' markets that grows them, chefs find myriad ways to use the fruits, for example, in galettes and chutneys, or cooked in syrup. Poaching turns quince a beautiful rosy hue and allows the subtle flavour to shine through. Because this is a simple dessert, the quality of the ricotta is important. Look for fresh ricotta and seek out sheep's milk ricotta if you can find it. Old Chatham Sheepherding Company, in the Hudson River Valley, makes a particularly delicate sheep's milk ricotta (page 62).

30 g (1 oz) shelled, unsalted, raw pistachio nuts

4 large quinces, about 1 kg (2 lb) total weight

375 ml (12 fl oz) lavender honey

1 teaspoon whole cloves

4 star anise

1 cinnamon stick

Peel of 1 lemon, cut into wide strips

250 g (½ lb) fresh ricotta cheese, preferably sheep's milk (see note)

Makes 4 servings

1 Preheat the oven to 180°C (350°F). Spread the pistachio nuts on a baking sheet and toast until fragrant and lightly browned, about 10 minutes. Pour on to a plate, let cool and then chop coarsely.

2 Peel the quinces, reserving the peels. Cut each quince into quarters and remove the core, making sure to remove all of it. Place the quince quarters in a large saucepan. Add the honey, cloves, star anise, cinnamon stick, and 1 l (1 ¾ pints) water. Place the quince peels and lemon peel on a 15-cm (6-inch) square of muslin, bring up the corners, and tie together with kitchen string. Add the muslin bundle to the pan, bring to a simmer over medium-high heat, reduce the heat to low, cover, and poach the quinces until tender, 15–20 minutes.

3 Remove and discard the muslin bundle. Using a slotted spoon, transfer the quince quarters to a bowl. Raise the heat to high and cook the poaching liquid until syrupy and reduced by half, about 5 minutes. Let cool to room temperature.

4 Divide the ricotta among 4 shallow bowls. Place 4 quince quarters around each mound of ricotta. Drizzle the poaching liquid, including the whole spices, over the quinces and ricotta. Garnish with the pistachios, dividing evenly, and serve at once.

Serve with a rich, late-harvest Gewürztraminer.

STRAWBERRY-RHUBARB CRISP WITH BUTTERMILK ICE CREAM

Every April, after a long, cold winter, New Yorkers are delighted to find the first two harbingers of spring at farmers' markets: cherry blossom branches and piles of rhubarb stalks. Rhubarb, also called pieplant, is almost exclusively cooked like fruit. In fact, in 1947, the U.S. Customs Court in Buffalo, New York, changed its designation from vegetable to fruit. Since strawberry season follows rhubarb by a few weeks, you can also make the crumble using 1.75 kg (3½ pounds) rhubarb and an extra 60 g (2 oz) granulated sugar.

1 To make the ice cream, in a heavy saucepan over medium-low heat, warm the cream. In a bowl, whisk together the egg yolks and granulated sugar. Slowly whisk half of the warm cream into the egg mixture, then pour it back into the pan, whisking constantly. Cook over medium-low heat, stirring constantly, until the custard thickens, about 5 minutes. Do not let the mixture boil. Remove from the heat, add the butter and salt and stir until the butter has melted. Stir in the buttermilk. Strain through a fine-mesh sieve into a bowl. Cover with clingfilm, pressing it on the custard to prevent a skin from forming. Refrigerate overnight.

2 Pour the custard into an ice-cream maker and freeze according to the manufacturer's instructions. Transfer the ice cream to a freezer-safe container. Cover and freeze until firm.

3 To make the crumble, preheat the oven to 180°C (375°F). Line a baking sheet with non-stick baking paper or aluminium foil. In a bowl, stir together 125 g (4 oz) of the flour, the brown sugar, oats, cinnamon, and cloves. Scatter the butter over the dry ingredients and, using your fingers, work it into the dry ingredients until they are moist but still crumbly.

4 In a 23- or 25-cm (9- or 10-inch) baking dish, stir together the rhubarb, strawberries, granulated sugar, and remaining 30 g (1 oz) flour. Spread out evenly in the dish. Sprinkle the topping evenly over the fruit. Place the dish on the prepared baking sheet and bake until the topping is golden and the fruit is bubbling, 40–50 minutes. Let cool slightly, then serve with the ice cream.

FOR THE ICE CREAM

250 ml (8 fl oz) double cream

6 medium egg yolks

250 g (8 oz) granulated sugar

2 tablespoons unsalted butter, cut into small pieces

½ teaspoon sea salt or fleur de sel

500 ml (16 fl oz) buttermilk

FOR THE CRUMBLE TOPPING

155 g (5 oz) plain flour

220 g (7 oz) firmly packed golden brown sugar

90 g (3 oz) rolled oats

½ teaspoon ground cinnamon

Pinch of ground cloves

185 g (6 oz) unsalted butter, cut into small pieces

1 kg (2 lb) rhubarb, cut horizontally into pieces 2 cm (¾ inch) thick

450 g (1 lb) strawberries, hulled and halved

250 g (8 oz) granulated sugar

Makes 8 servings

Ice Cream

No flavour is left unturned when it comes to ice cream. The trend started in the 1990s, when Ciao Bella founder Jon Snyder began churning custom flavours for some of New York City's best chefs. Today, vanilla is a rarity. Tarts, tortes, and crumbles are more likely to be topped with maple ice cream at Craft, sweetened condensed milk ice cream at Spice Market, or honey ice cream at Babbo.

New Yorkers also enjoy the ritual of going out for an ice cream after dinner. In Chinatown, they stop at the Chinatown Ice Cream Factory for flavours such as ginger, lychee and almond cookie, and at Cones in Greenwich Village for *dulce de leche* and tiramisù. Neighbourhood institutions including Hinsch's on the Upper East Side, Eggers Ice Cream Parlor in Staten Island, and Eddie's Sweet Shop in Queens attract patrons returning for sundaes, sodas, and milk shakes. At the Brooklyn Ice Cream Factory, located in a 1920s fireboat house, owner Mark Thompson has set out to make rich Philadelphia-style ice cream using the best ingredients. Every pint is hand-packed, and the focus is on basic flavours, including peach and vanilla.

BLUEBERRY SORBET AND ICE CREAM WITH BROWN SUGAR COOKIES

In 1984, when only nineteen, Jon F. Snyder founded Ciao Bella. In 2002, thirteen years after selling it, he opened another ice-cream company in a little shop on the Lower East Side. At Il Laboratorio del Gelato, which he thinks of as a "custom lab", he makes ice creams and sorbets using a single machine. Snyder is best known for supplying restaurants such as Pastis, Barbuto, and Mary's Fish Camp with custom flavours. He avoids using eggs in fruit-flavoured ice creams because he wants the fruit to dominate. For this blueberry sorbet, he strains only some of the mixture, which ensures a richly coloured dessert.

FOR THE SORBET

90 g (3 oz) granulated sugar

450 g (1 lb) blueberries

FOR THE ICE CREAM

160 ml (5 fl oz) double cream

375 ml (12 fl oz) single cream

125 g (4 oz) granulated sugar plus 1 teaspoon

1 teaspoon peach or apricot jam

310 g (10 oz) blueberries

FOR THE BISCUITS

250 g (8 oz) unsalted butter, at room temperature

220 g (7 oz) firmly packed golden brown sugar

½ teaspoon pure vanilla extract

315 g (10 oz) plain flour, plus more for dusting

½ teaspoon ground cinnamon

¼ teaspoon salt

2 tablespoons turbinado or barbados sugar

Makes 1 l (1¾ pints) each sorbet and ice cream, and 30 biscuits

1 To make the sorbet, in a saucepan over medium heat, combine the granulated sugar and 60 ml (2 fl oz) water. Bring to the boil, stirring to dissolve the sugar. Transfer the sugar syrup to a bowl, cover and refrigerate until chilled, at least 1 hour.

2 Place the blueberries and 2 tablespoons of the chilled syrup in a blender or food processor and purée thoroughly. Reserve 125 ml (4 fl oz) of the blueberry mixture. Strain the remainder through a fine-mesh sieve set over a bowl, pressing on the mixture with the back of a spoon. Add the reserved blueberry mixture and the remaining syrup and stir to combine. Cover and refrigerate overnight. Pour into an ice-cream maker and freeze according to the manufacturer's instructions. Transfer the sorbet to a freezer-safe container. Cover and freeze until firm.

3 To make the ice cream, in a heavy saucepan over medium heat, combine the double cream, single cream, 125 g (4 oz) granulated sugar and jam. Bring to a simmer and cook until the sugar dissolves, 10 minutes. Do not allow the mixture to boil. Strain through a fine-mesh sieve set over a bowl. Cover with clingfilm, pressing it directly on the custard to prevent a skin from forming and refrigerate overnight.

4 Place 60 g (2 oz) of the blueberries in a freezer-safe container and freeze until just firm, about 1 hour. Remove from the freezer and chop the berries coarsely, roughly quartering them. Place in a bowl, sprinkle with the 1 teaspoon granulated sugar, and set aside. Place the remaining 250 g (8 oz) blueberries in

a blender or food processor and purée thoroughly. Strain through a fine-mesh sieve set over a bowl, pressing on the mixture with the back of a spoon. Add the chilled custard and chopped frozen blueberries, and stir to combine. Pour into an ice-cream maker and freeze according to the manufacturer's instructions. Transfer the ice cream to a freezer-safe container. Cover and freeze until firm.

5 To make the biscuits, preheat the oven to 160°C (325°F). Line a baking sheet with non-stick baking paper. In a bowl, using an electric mixer on high speed, cream the butter with the brown sugar until fluffy, about 3 minutes. Scrape down the sides of the bowl, then beat in the vanilla. In another bowl, stir together the flour, cinnamon, and salt. Add to the butter mixture and, with the mixer on low speed, mix until the flour is no longer visible and the dough is smooth.

6 Dust your hands with flour. Scoop up 1 tablespoon of dough and roll it into a ball. Place on the prepared baking sheet. Repeat to form the remaining biscuits, placing them at least 5 cm (2 inches) apart. Use the palm of your hand to flatten each dough ball into a disc 9 mm (⅓ inch) thick. Sprinkle the biscuits generously with the turbinado sugar. Bake until the biscuits are slightly crusty to the touch and the bottoms are golden, about 30 minutes. Remove from the oven and cool on the baking sheet for 5 minutes. Transfer to a wire rack to cool.

7 Place scoops of the sorbet and ice cream in a serving bowl. Serve with the biscuits.

BRIOCHE ROLLS

PLU: 0246

Citarella

.95 ea.

BANANA-WALNUT BREAD PUDDING

An old-fashioned dessert that uses day-old bread, bread pudding can be made in so many ways that it can seem like an entirely different dish from one place to another. At diners and Jewish delis, the pudding is often dense and heavy. At smart restaurants, delicate versions are baked in individual dishes and served as French pain perdu, *topped with caramelised fruit and crème anglaise. No matter what the restaurant, egg-enriched brioche and challah are favourites for making bread pudding and are recommended for this version, which is moist inside with a crunchy top.*

1 Preheat the oven to 180°C (350°F). Lightly butter a 25-cm (10-inch) soufflé dish or other round baking dish with at least 5-cm (2-inch) sides.

2 Place the bread cubes in a large bowl. In another bowl, whisk together the eggs, butter, sugars, cinnamon, nutmeg, and salt until combined. Whisk in the cream, milk, and vanilla. Pour over the bread cubes and toss to coat evenly. Let stand until the bread has absorbed as much of the liquid as possible, about 15 minutes.

3 Meanwhile, spread the walnut pieces on a baking sheet and toast until fragrant and lightly browned, about 10 minutes. Pour on to a plate, let cool and then coarsely chop.

4 Add the walnuts and bananas to the bread mixture and toss gently to combine. Pour into the prepared dish. Bake until the pudding is set and the top is golden brown and slightly crisp, 70–80 minutes. Serve warm.

Serve with a nutty, sweet white port.

375 g (12 oz) day-old challah, brioche, or crusty French round, cut into 2.5-cm (1-inch) cubes, thickest crusts removed

4 medium eggs

125 g (4 oz) unsalted butter, melted

185 g (6 oz) granulated sugar

185 g (6 oz) firmly packed golden brown sugar

2 teaspoons ground cinnamon

½ teaspoon freshly grated nutmeg

1 teaspoon sea salt

500 ml (16 fl oz) double cream

500 ml (16 fl oz) full-cream milk

1 tablespoon pure vanilla extract

125 g (4 oz) walnut pieces

450 g (1 lb) ripe bananas, peeled and cut into 2-cm (¾-inch) slices

Makes 8 servings

DEVIL'S FOOD CUPCAKES WITH VANILLA BUTTERCREAM

With all its fancy patisseries and ethnic bakeries, who would have thought that the cupcake, the icon of American childhood birthday parties, would become the dessert darling of New York City? It all started with the Cupcake Café, on an otherwise Italian stretch of Hell's Kitchen, which turns out beautiful cupcakes decorated with brightly-coloured flowers. Buttercup Bake Shop on the Upper East Side is also a favourite for cupcakes. But nothing compares to the popularity of Magnolia Bakery, where the queue stretches out of the door.

1 Preheat the oven to 180°C (350°F). Line 12 deep muffin cups with paper liners or lightly butter the muffin cups and the top of the muffin tin.

2 In a bowl, combine the cocoa powder, brown sugar, and coffee powder. Add the boiling water, stir until smooth and let cool to room temperature. Stir in the buttermilk and vanilla. Set aside.

3 In a large bowl, using an electric mixer on high speed, beat together the butter and sugar until fluffy and almost white in colour, 3–4 minutes. Add the eggs, one at a time, beating well and scraping down the bowl after each addition. In a separate bowl, stir together the flour, bicarbonate, and salt. Fold one-third of the chocolate mixture into the beaten butter. Add one-third of the flour mixture, stirring gently to combine. Continue folding in the chocolate mixture and adding the flour until all the mixtures are combined into a smooth batter.

4 Divide the batter evenly among the muffin cups. Bake until a toothpick inserted into the centre of a cupcake comes out clean, 15–18 minutes. Let cool to room temperature in the pan on a wire rack.

5 To make the buttercream, in a bowl, using an electric mixer on high speed, beat the butter until fluffy, 3–4 minutes. Add the egg yolks and beat until fluffy. Beat in the vanilla, salt, and icing sugar.

6 Remove the cupcakes from the tin. Spread the buttercream evenly over the top of each cupcake using an icing spatula.

45 g (1½ oz) Dutch cocoa powder (such as Van Houten)

185 g (6 oz) firmly packed golden brown sugar

2 teaspoons instant coffee powder

250 ml (8 fl oz) boiling water

125 ml (4 fl oz) buttermilk

2 teaspoons pure vanilla extract

125 g (4 oz) unsalted butter, at room temperature

185 g (6 oz) granulated sugar

2 medium eggs, at room temperature

200 g (6½ oz) plain flour

1½ teaspoons bicarbonate of soda

½ teaspoon salt

FOR THE BUTTERCREAM

250 g (8 oz) unsalted butter, at room temperature

2 large egg yolks

1 tablespoon pure vanilla extract

¼ teaspoon salt

250 g (8 oz) icing sugar

Makes 12 cupcakes

Chocolate

With their collective sweet tooth and willingness to indulge, New Yorkers appreciate nothing so much as a top-quality chocolate. Stopping at Li-Lac Chocolates in Greenwich Village is a neighbourhood ritual. Before any public holiday, locals line up outside the quaint, lilac-painted store, where confections have been made on the premises since 1923, for chocolate-covered creams and festive season specialities. In Morningside Heights, Columbia University students and lecturers squeeze into Mondel's Homemade Chocolates, owned by the same family since 1944, for chocolate-covered nut barks, turtles, and other treats.

Those looking for a refined chocolate experience appreciate the truffles made by Francois Payard, once the pastry chef at the Daniel restaurant, who sells chocolates at his East Side patisserie. Jacques Torres, his protégé, has created a house of chocolate worship in Brooklyn, where customers drink cups of hot chocolate and eat chocolate-covered salted caramels. Pushing the limits further, Chocolate Bar in Greenwich Village offers a tasting of five chocolates.

RUSTIC APPLE TART

From November, when the last of the pears and Concord grapes have been harvested, until May, when the first strawberries appear, apples are the only fruit found at local farmers' markets. More than a hundred varieties come from the Hudson River Valley, Lake Champlain Valley and southern Lake Ontario shore. One of these, the Northern Spy, was developed in the New York town of East Bloomfield in 1800. It is sometimes called the northern pie apple because of its sharp flavour and its ability to hold its shape when baked. Granny Smith or Newtown pippins are also good choices for this rustic tart.

FOR THE PASTRY

280 g (9 oz) plain flour

90 g (3 oz) granulated sugar

½ teaspoon salt

185 g (6 oz) cold unsalted butter, cut into small cubes

2 large egg yolks

2 tablespoons ice water, or as needed

1.5 kg (3 lb) tart baking apples (see note), peeled, cored, and cut into slices 9 mm (⅓ inch) thick

Juice of ½ lemon

185 g (6 oz) granulated sugar

½ teaspoon salt

½ teaspoon ground cinnamon

Pinch of freshly grated nutmeg

45 g (1½ oz) plain flour

1 large egg yolk beaten with 1 tablespoon double cream

Coarse sugar for sprinkling

2 tablespoons unsalted butter, cut into small cubes

Makes one 23-cm (9-inch) tart, or 8 servings

1 To make the pastry by hand, in a large bowl, stir together the flour, granulated sugar, and salt. Scatter the butter over the dry ingredients and, using a pastry cutter or 2 knives, cut in the butter until the mixture forms coarse crumbs the size of large peas. In a small bowl, whisk together the egg yolks and 2 tablespoons of ice water. Drizzle it over the flour mixture and stir with a fork until evenly moistened, adding more water, a few drops at a time, if needed. Alternatively, to make the pastry in a food processor, combine the flour, sugar, and salt and pulse to blend. Add the butter and pulse until the mixture forms coarse crumbs the size of large peas. In a small bowl, whisk together the egg yolks and 2 tablespoons ice water. Add to the flour mixture and pulse just until the dough begins to come together, adding more water, a few drops at a time, if needed.

2 Transfer the dough to a sheet of clingfilm and shape it into a disc 2 cm (¾ inch) thick. Wrap tightly in the clingfilm and refrigerate for 1 hour or up to overnight.

3 Preheat the oven to 180°C (375°F). Line a large baking sheet with non-stick baking paper. In a bowl, combine the apples, lemon juice, granulated sugar, salt, cinnamon, nutmeg, and 2 tablespoons of the flour. Toss to coat the apples.

4 On a lightly floured work surface, roll out the dough disc into a round 28–30 cm (11–12 inches) in diameter and about 6 mm (¼ inch) thick, dusting the rolling pin lightly with flour to prevent sticking. Drape the dough over the rolling pin and lay it on the prepared baking sheet. Sprinkle the dough with the remaining 2 tablespoons flour, leaving a 5-cm (2-inch) border uncovered. Mound the apple mixture on top of the flour. Fold the uncovered border of dough up and over the apple filling, forming loose pleats all around the filling and leaving the centre open. Brush the pleated dough with the egg mixture and sprinkle with coarse sugar. Dot the filling with the butter cubes.

5 Bake until the apples are bubbling and tender when pierced with the tip of a knife and the crust is golden brown, 50–60 minutes. Serve the tart warm, cut into wedges.

Serve with a late-harvest Vignoles with apple flavours, such as Swedish Hill from the Finger Lakes or with a French dessert wine such as Château d'Yquem.

SWEET POTATO PIE WITH MAPLE WHIPPED CREAM

Harlem, settled by the Dutch in the 1600s, became an African-American enclave in the 1920s, when the housing market collapsed. To fill empty flats, landlords appealed to the scores of African-Americans leaving the southern states in search of a better life. Since the 1980s, Harlem has undergone a rebirth, attracting tourists who come to see the historic architecture and eat in restaurants such as Sylvia's and Miss Mamie's Spoonbread, Too. Most serve southern-style home cooking such as pulled pork and black-eyed peas. Along with peach cobbler and bread pudding, sweet potato pie is an essential menu item.

1 To make the pastry by hand, in a large bowl, stir together the flour and salt. Scatter the butter and shortening over the dry ingredients and, using a pastry cutter or 2 knives, cut in the butter and shortening until the mixture forms coarse crumbs the size of large peas. Drizzle the 2 tablespoons ice water over the flour mixture and stir with a fork until evenly moistened, adding more water only if needed for the dough to come together. Alternatively, to make the pastry in a food processor, combine the flour and salt and pulse to blend. Add the butter and shortening and pulse until the mixture forms coarse crumbs the size of large peas. Add the 2 tablespoons ice water and pulse just until the dough begins to come together, adding more water only if needed for the dough to come together.

2 Transfer the dough to a sheet of clingfilm and shape it into a disc 2 cm (¾ inch) thick. Wrap tightly in the clingfilm and refrigerate for 1 hour or up to overnight.

3 To make the filling, bring a large saucepan of water to the boil over high heat. Add the sweet potatoes and boil until very tender, about 30 minutes. Drain well and set aside to cool. When the potatoes are cool enough to handle, pass the flesh through a ricer into a large bowl or purée in a food processor until smooth and then transfer to a large bowl. Cover and refrigerate until needed.

4 On a lightly floured work surface, roll out the dough disc into a round 30 cm (12 inches) in diameter and 3 mm (⅛ inch) thick. Drape the dough over the rolling pin and transfer it to a 23-cm (9-inch) pie tin, easing it into the bottom and sides. Trim the overhang so it extends 2 cm (¾ inch) beyond the rim of the tin. Roll the overhang under to shape a high edge that rests on top of the rim. Crimp around the rim and refrigerate for 30 minutes.

5 Preheat the oven to 180°C (350°F). Line the pie shell with a large piece of aluminium foil, fill with pie weights, uncooked rice or dried beans, and bake until the crust dries slightly and the foil can be removed easily, about 15 minutes. Carefully remove the weights and foil, and continue to bake until the crust is set, about 5 minutes longer.

6 To finish the filling, add the cream, eggs, maple syrup, and vanilla extract to the puréed sweet potatoes and whisk until smooth. In a small bowl, combine the sugar, flour, salt, ginger, cinnamon, and ¼ teaspoon nutmeg. Add to the sweet potato mixture and whisk until smooth. Pour the filling into the warm, partially baked pie shell. Bake until the filling is firm around the edges and slightly jiggly in the centre (it will continue to set when removed from the oven), 50–60 minutes. Transfer to a wire rack to cool.

7 To make the whipped cream, pour the cream and maple syrup into a chilled bowl. Using an electric mixer on high speed, beat until the cream forms medium peaks. To serve, cut the pie into wedges and top each wedge with a dollop of whipped cream. Sprinkle with freshly grated nutmeg, if desired.

FOR THE PASTRY

315 g (10 oz) plain flour

1 teaspoon salt

250 g (8 oz) cold unsalted butter, cut into small cubes

60 g (2 oz) vegetable shortening

2 tablespoons ice water

FOR THE FILLING

750 g (1½ lb) orange-fleshed sweet potatoes, peeled and cut into chunks

250 ml (8 fl oz) double cream

3 medium eggs, lightly beaten

60 ml (2 fl oz) maple syrup

1 teaspoon pure vanilla extract

250 g (8 oz) sugar

1 tablespoon plain flour

1 teaspoon salt

½ teaspoon *each* ground ginger and cinnamon

¼ teaspoon grated nutmeg, plus more for garnish (optional)

250 ml (8 fl oz) double cream

2 tablespoons maple syrup

Makes 8 servings

GLOSSARY

ASIAN CHILLI OIL A staple of Asian cuisine, now finding its way into Western kitchens, chilli oil is made by infusing heated peanut or corn oil with dried chilli flakes. Drops of chilli oil are used to add spicy flavour to many stir-fries and sautés. Stored oil will become more fiery over time. It is available in Asian markets and gourmet food shops.

ASIAN SESAME OIL A fragrant, deep amber oil made by extracting oil from roasted sesame seeds. It is used primarily in Japan, Korea, and China, where it is employed as a flavouring rather than as a cooking oil.

BALSAMIC VINEGAR The celebrated vinegar of Modena, Italy, is made by ageing the pure wine must (unfermented grape juice) of Trebbiano grapes from 1 year to more than 75 years. Younger vinegars are added to salad dressings and glazes; more costly, syrupy, long-aged vinegars are used in small amounts as a flavouring. White balsamic vinegar, made when the "must" is not caramelised, will not colour dressings or sauces. It may be difficult to find; look for it in gourmet food shops or online sources.

BEANS Long a garden staple, fresh beans fall into two categories, those eaten in the pod and those that have to be shelled before eating.

POD BEANS, also called runner beans, snap beans, string beans, green beans, and French beans are consumed whole (outer pod and inner seeds). The taste is mild and fresh with grassy overtones. Purchase evenly green pods that look as though they will snap decisively when broken.

SHELL BEANS are available in their fresh state in the spring and summer in farmers' markets and greengrocers. Only the inner seeds are consumed; the pods are discarded. Varieties include adzuki, appaloosa, cannellini, flageolet, butter beans, and broad beans. Broad beans, one of the more popular shell beans, have a faintly bitter flavour.

BEEF MARROW BONES Although marrow is often eaten in its own right as a delicacy, the bones are used to make a rich stock and to flavour soups, stews, or sauces. Most often from the leg, but sometimes from the spine, marrow bones are available from good butchers (who sometimes will give them for free to good customers) and some supermarkets.

CHICORY Also known as Belgian endive or witloof, it has white (or sometimes red-tipped), tightly furled, bullet-shaped heads that have a bittersweet taste. It is grown in the dark and tends to become bitter when exposed to light. It should be refrigerated and used within a day after purchase.

BROCCOLI RABE A pleasantly bitter Italian vegetable related to cabbage and mustard. The long, thin stalks terminate in small yellow florets and have slender leaves with jagged edges. Also known as broccoli raab, *cima di rape*, and *rapini*.

BUTTERNUT SQUASH A large, long winter squash identifiable by the round bulb at one end. It has beige skin and orange-yellow flesh.

TO SEED BUTTERNUT SQUASH, use a heavy, sharp knife to open the squash by cutting it in half. If the skin is very hard, securely wedge the knife in the squash, then use a wooden kitchen mallet to carefully tap the knife. Scrape out all seeds and fibres with a sharp-edged spoon.

CALVADOS This dry apple brandy aged in oak comes from Normandy, where apples are plentiful. It is named after the region in which it is made.

CELERIAC The knobby root of a celery plant (a cousin to the familiar celery bunches) grown specifically for its root. Celeriac has a similar, though more pronounced, flavour than celery. Once the brown bulb is peeled, its tender ivory flesh can be shredded for salads or cooked and puréed.

CHANTERELLE MUSHROOM A subtly flavoured, pale yellow, trumpet-shaped mushroom about 5–7.5 cm (2–3 inches) in length. Chanterelles grow in the wild and are cultivated commercially.

CHILLI PEPPERS Over centuries of domestication, hundreds of chilli pepper varieties have been developed. Requiring hot summers, they grow well in tropical regions and can be large or tiny, mild or fiery. Native to South America.

JALAPEÑO Ranging from mildly hot to fiery, the fleshy jalapeño is usually green but can also be red. It measures 5–10 cm (2–4 inches) in length and is sold fresh, canned, or pickled. Use in place of other chillies, such as serrano or Thai. Substitute 2 or 3 jalapeños for 1 habañero or Scotch bonnet.

SCOTCH BONNET An extremely hot chilli, smaller than the habanero at only 2.5–4 cm (1–1½ inches) long. The little round fresh chillies, from the Caribbean, are green, yellow, orange, or red.

CHINESE EGG NOODLES Much like Italian egg pasta, Chinese egg noodles are cut or extruded from a dough of wheat flour, eggs, and salt. The noodles vary in size, and are available dried or fresh. They are sometimes artificially "egg-flavoured" and are so labelled on packets.

CLAM JUICE The strained liquid of shucked clams, possessing a refreshing briny flavour. It is sold in the seafood department of grocers specialising in American food.

CLAMS These molluscs, also called bivalves, are either hard-shelled or soft-shelled. Distinct varieties are found in the Atlantic and the Pacific. Be sure to buy the freshest clams possible from a reputable market. Store on a flat tray or in a shallow bowl, cover with a damp cloth and refrigerate for no more than 2 days. For the best results, serve clams the same day you buy them. Cockles can be substituted.

CHERRYSTONE A small, hard-shelled Atlantic clam, measuring up to 7.5 cm (3 inches) in diameter. Cherrystones are delicious raw or cooked.

LITTLENECK There are two kinds of these hard-shelled clams. The smaller Atlantic littlenecks are particularly sweet and delicious raw or very gently cooked. Pacific littlenecks are not related and should be steamed as they can be somewhat tough.

MANILA Also called Japanese clam. A small, sweet clam not native to the United States and farmed off the Pacific coast. Usually harvested when barely 2.5 cm (1 inch) in diameter, manila clams are favourites among chefs and can be served raw or steamed.

QUAHOG Pronounced "coe-hog". A large, hard-shelled clam from the Atlantic, measuring 7.5 cm (3 inches) in diameter. The flavour is sweet, but not as sweet and salty as smaller hard-shelled clams.

FENNEL The bulb, stems, and fronds of the fennel plant have a sweet, aniseed flavour and can be eaten raw or cooked. Also known as *finocchio*.

FETA CHEESE A young sheep's milk cheese, traditionally made in Greece, Bulgaria, and Corsica and pickled in a brine. Feta has a pleasant salty flavour and a crumbly texture. American, Australian, Danish, and German feta cheeses are often made from cow's milk but taste much like sheep's milk feta. Feta may also be made from goat's milk.

FOIE GRAS The rich, buttery liver of a goose or duck, traditionally part of French cuisine. Look for *foie gras frais*, which is lightly cooked (pasteurised). It should be an even beige, have a smooth surface, be slightly firm to the touch, and have a fresh smell. Recent European Union legislation is attempting to ban it on grounds of cruelty to animals so it is becoming harder to find.

GRAND MARNIER A popular orange-flavoured liqueur, distinguished by its pure Cognac base.

HARISSA A spicy, red Tunisian sauce made from chilli peppers, garlic, and spices such as coriander and caraway, combined with olive oil. *Harissa* enlivens many dishes, including stews and soups. Look for the sauce in Middle Eastern grocers.

JERUSALEM ARTICHOKE A tuberous vegetable native to North America which resembles a small, knobby potato. Although its subtle flavour is reminiscent of the artichoke, the two vegetables are not related. The name is believed to derive from the Italian *girasole*, "sunflower", a plant to which it is related. Also called sunchoke.

LAMB'S LETTUCE Also known as lamb's quarters and mâche, this salad green grows in small, loose bunches and is harvested in early spring. It was once a weed growing in wheatfields. The oval leaves are delicate and mild in flavour.

MALTED MILK POWDER A mixture of powdered milk and malt sugar, which is derived from barley. Traditionally used in desserts, Ovaltine or Horlicks can be substituted.

MASCARPONE A fresh Italian cheese made from cream and rich in flavour, has a soft, smooth texture. Mascarpone is sold in plastic tubs in the cheese section of Italian groceries and in good supermarkets. It is used in many savoury and sweet dishes.

MATZO MEAL A fine-textured meal ground from matzo, Jewish unleavened bread. It is the main ingredient in matzo balls and is also used in baking, as a coating for fried foods, and as a thickener. It comes in three grades, fine, medium, and coarse.

MIRIN An important ingredient in Japanese cuisine, mirin is a sweet cooking wine made by fermenting glutinous rice and sugar. It adds a rich flavour to sauces, dressings, and simmered dishes.

MISO A thick, rich-tasting paste fermented from cooked soy beans, wheat or rice and salt. The two most common forms are the robust red miso (*aka miso*) and the milder white miso (*shiro miso*). Miso is mostly used as a seasoning in Japanese cooking and is available in good supermarkets.

MOREL MUSHROOM The morel is distinguished by a long, oval cap covered with a network of deep crevices and by an intense musky aroma. As grit and dirt are easily trapped in the honeycombed caps, morels need to be immersed briefly in cold water and a little white vinegar, then drained and dried with a kitchen towel before using. They can also be bought dried from gourmet shops.

ONION, PEARL A pungent onion about 2 cm (³⁄₄ inch) in diameter, often added whole to stewed and braised dishes. Also known as pickling onion.

TO PEEL PEARL ONIONS, immerse them in boiling water for about 1 minute, then drain well and let cool. Use a small, sharp knife to trim off the root ends. Slip off the skins by squeezing each onion gently with your fingers.

ONIONS, SWEET Most fresh onions are sweet and moist, but certain varieties are appreciated for their exceptional sweetness and juiciness. Mild in flavour, these onions are known by the names of the places where they are grown, and because of their soil and climate requirements, they lose their characteristic sweetness if grown outside their place of origin. Vidalia onions, from Georgia, come into season during the spring; Walla Walla onions, from Washington, are available in late summer.

PANCETTA Spiced and cured, but not smoked, Italian bacon made by rubbing a slab of pork belly with a mixture of spices, then rolling it into a tight cylinder and curing it for at least 2 months. Pancetta has a moist, silky texture and is typically sold in thin slices in butcher's and Italian delicatessens.

PAPRIKA, HUNGARIAN Made from ground dried red peppers, paprika can be sweet, semi-sweet, or hot and ranges in colour from orange-red to deep red. The spice is produced in Hungary and Spain, as well as in South America and California; paprika from Hungary, however, is thought to be the finest.

PÂTÉ Typically a rich, finely minced meat mixture, pâté can be made from almost any meat or mixture of meat, the most common being pork, veal, and rabbit, as well as chicken liver and foie gras. Some mixtures are smooth, others are chunky and still others are studded with a variety of ingredients.

PECORINO ROMANO CHEESE A pleasantly salty Italian sheep's milk cheese with a grainy texture. Primarily used for grating or shaving.

PHYLLO Large, paper-thin sheets of dough that, when baked, result in flaky layers of pastry. Commonly used in Middle Eastern and Greek preparations, both sweet and savoury. Also spelled "filo".

PICKLES, BREAD-AND-BUTTER Made from pickling a thinly sliced, unpeeled cucumber in a brine containing onion, mustard, celery seeds, cloves, and turmeric and sweetened with sugar.

PINE NUT The small, pale seed of certain varieties of pine tree, with a rich, sweet, slightly resinous flavour. Much used in southern European and Middle Eastern cooking, pine nuts appear in savoury dishes such as rice dishes, salads, and sauces as well as in pastries and desserts.

POLENTA The term refers both to cornmeal cooked in a generous amount of liquid until it thickens and becomes tender and also to the ground cornmeal used to make the signature Italian dish. Polenta may be yellow or white and either coarsely or finely ground. The classic version is made from coarsely ground yellow maize.

POTATO, FINGERLING First introduced at farmers' markets by growers aiming at the gourmet niche, these thin-skinned, dense, waxy potatoes are slender and elongated in shape, hence their name. They are often served roasted with olive oil, salt, and herbs, which enhances their sweet, creamy texture.

PRUNE The *pruneau d'Agen,* a variety of prunes grown for centuries in the Agen district of Bordeaux, France, is the best. Now it is grown in California, the origin of most of the dried plums sold in the United States. Dried plums are often paired with meat in savoury dishes.

PUFF PASTRY A light, flaky pastry that is made by layering butter and pastry dough to form hundreds of thin, crisp leaves that puff up in the heat of the oven. Fresh or frozen puff dough is often available at quality bakeries and supermarkets.

RADICCHIO A variety of chicory native to Italy with variegated purple-red leaves that are sturdy and moderately bitter. Eaten cooked or raw, radicchio is sold at farmers' markets and most well-stocked supermarkets.

RAMPIONS This intensely flavoured onion with a garlicky edge grows wild. Also known as ramps, they are harvested in late spring, and their season is brief; therefore, spring onions, Welsh onions or small leeks may be used in their place. Look for rampions in farmers' markets. Choose specimens with broad, firm, bright-green leaves.

RHUBARB The reddish pink, celery-like stalks of rhubarb, though technically a vegetable, are commonly used in crumbles, pies, tarts, and pre-serves. Inedible raw, rhubarb has a tart flavour that is transformed when cooked with sugar. Be sure to remove the leaves before using, as they contain oxalic acid and are poisonous. Hothouse-grown rhubarb is available year-round in some areas; field-grown rhubarb appears in April and May.

SAKE Although commonly thought of as Japanese rice wine, this aromatic, dry, clear, 30° proof liquid is actually brewed like beer. It is used in cooking or is served to accompany a meal.

SCALLOP, BAY The most highly prized of all scal-lops in the U.S., measuring about 12 mm (½ inch) in diameter and characterised by a sweet, delicate flavour. Bay scallops are harvested from a small region of the Atlantic Ocean and are rarely found outside of East Coast fish markets during their short season, which begins in October and continues

through March. Local Peconic Bay scallops, from Long Island, are a regional New York favourite. In the U.S., scallops are not usually sold on the shell.

SKATE An ancient fish classified as a "ray", skate is caught in the Atlantic Ocean off the Northeast region of the United States in spring and autumn. The fins provide pale, firm, somewhat sweet-tasting flesh that has an inherent ammonia scent. To eliminate this odour, soak the flesh in water containing a bit of vinegar, lemon, or lime juice.

SOFT-SHELLED CRABS Blue crabs have hard shells that they shed several times before they reach full maturity. During the days before they grow new, larger hard shells, they are known as soft-shelled crabs. Available from the spring to early autumn, the crabs are eaten whole, soft shell and all.

STAR ANISE This star-shaped, seed-bearing pod has an aniseed flavour but comes from a Chinese evergreen tree related to the magnolia. It is used extensively in Chinese and Indian cookery.

TAHINI A rich, creamy paste made from ground sesame seeds possessing a subtle sesame flavour and smooth texture. Tahini is sold in jars or cans. After opening a container, stir the tahini well before using and refrigerate the remainder for up to 2 months. It is used in Middle Eastern dishes.

TOMATOES Classified as a fruit, tomatoes are generally treated as a vegetable. They come in a variety of sizes and colours and are eaten both raw and cooked in cuisines worldwide.

PEELING AND SEEDING A TOMATO Cut a shallow X in the blossom end of the tomato. Immerse in a pan of boiling water until the peel begins to curl away from the X, about 30 seconds. Transfer to a bowl of ice water to cool, then peel away the skin. To seed, cut the tomato in half horizontally and squeeze each half gently to dislodge the seeds.

TRUFFLE A strongly aromatic fungus found in France and Italy and prized by chefs and gourmets worldwide. Truffle oil is a good and inexpensive way to add the haunting fragrance to salads, pastas, and other dishes.

INGREDIENT SOURCES

D'ARTAGNAN

Hudson Valley foie gras pâté

(800) 327-8246

www.dartagnan.com

DEAN & DELUCA

Herbs, spices, oils, truffles, and mushrooms

(800) 692-3354

www.deandeluca.com

FISCHER BROS. & LESLIE BUTCHER

Kosher beef, lamb, poultry, and gourmet foods

(212) 787-1715

www.fischerbros.com

GORTON'S FRESH SEAFOOD

Black cod, clams, soft shell crab, Maine lobster, bay scallops, and skate

(800) 335-3674

www.gortonsfreshseafood.com

H&H BAGELS

New York bagels

(800) NY-BAGEL

www.hhbagels.com

JUNIOR'S

New York cheesecake

(800) 458-6467

www.juniorscheesecake.com

OLD CHATHAM SHEEPHERDING COMPANY

Artisanal cheeses

(800) 743-3760

www.blacksheepcheese.com

2ND AVENUE DELI

Kosher deli food, pickles, rye, and challah

(800) 692-3354

www.2ndavedeli.com

INDEX

ACKNOWLEDGMENTS

Carolynn Carreño would like to thank her agent, Janis Donnaud. From Weldon-Owen Publishing, she would like to thank Hannah Rahill for giving her the opportunity to work on such a challenging and rewarding project, and Kim Goodfriend, for her patience, keen editorial vision and impeccable feedback, all of which served to make this book the best it could be. Thanks to Christian Albin, Andy Arons, Daniel Boulud, Jimmy Bradley, Bruce and Eric Bromberg, John Doherty, Peter Hoffman, Sharon Lebewohl, Stanley Lobel, the Maccioni family, Waldy Malouf, Max McCalman, Rick Moonan, Julian Nicolini, Abram Orwasher, David Page, Bob Ransom, Mary Redding, Marcus Samuelsson, Jon F. Snyder, Bill Telepan, Jonathan Waxman, Eli Zabar, and the folks at Ess-a-Bagel, Murray's Cheese Shop, and Lombardi's Pizza for sharing their time and knowledge for the sake of getting it right.

Weldon Owen and the photography team, including Quentin Bacon and George Dolese, wish to extend their gratitude to the owners and workers of the restaurants, bakeries, shops, and other culinary businesses in New York who participated in this project: 2nd Ave Deli; 9th Avenue International Market; Artisanal Fromagerie & Bistro; Balthazar; Bar Jamon; Barney Greengrass; Bierkraft; Bill Telepan of the former JUdson Grill; Billy's Bakery; Bruce Bromberg and Eric Bromberg of Blue Ribbon Restaurant and the accommodating staff of Blue Ribbon Bakery; Café Angelique; Café Gitane; Ceci-Cela Patisserie; Chocolate Bar; Christian Albin and Julian and the staff of the Four Seasons Restaurant; City Bakery; Corrado Bread & Pastry; Cupcake Café; Daniel Boulud and the staff of Daniel and Café Boulud; DiPalo's Italian Deli; The Donut Plant; Ear Inn; Eli Zabar and the staff of the Vinegar Factory, E.A.T. Café, and Eli's Bread; Ess-a-Bagel; Faicco's (Italian Deli); Felix; Ferrara Gelati; Fischer Brothers & Leslie; Florent; Giorgione; Gramercy Tavern; Grand Central Market; Grimaldi's Pizza; Hallo Berlin Sausages; Havana-Chelsea Restaurant; Jacques Torres Chocolates; Jean-Georges Vongerichten and the staff of Jean Georges; Jimmy Bradley of the Red Cat; John Doherty of Oscar's American Brasserie at the Waldorf-Astoria; John's Pizza; Jon F. Snyder of Il Laboratorio del Gelato; Jonathan Waxman and the staff of Barbuto; Junior's; Katz's Delicatessen; Kelly and Ping Noodle Shop; Kossar's Bialys; Luna Restaurant; the Maccioni family of Osteria del Circo and Le Cirque 2000; Mario Batali and the staff of Babbo Ristorante e Enoteca, Bar Jamón, Lupa, and Otto Enoteca Pizzeria; Marcus Samuelsson of Aquavit; Mary Redding and the staff of Mary's Fish Camp; Meet Café; Moishe's Second Avenue Home Made Bakery; Moshe's Falafel; Nobu; Once Upon A Tart…; The Palm Steakhouse; Pastis; Peter Hoffman of Savoy Restaurant; Peter Luger's; Poseidon Greek Bakery; Relish; Rick Moonen of RM Restaurant; Schiller's Liquor Bar; Sea Breeze fish market; Smith & Wollensky; Sylvia's Restaurant; Michael Romano of Union Square Café; Union Square Greenmarket; Veselka Coffee Shop; Vintage New York wine shop; Waldy Malouf of Beacon Restaurant; and Yonah Schimmel's Knishery. A very special thank you to the staff of Murray's Cheese Shop, who went above and beyond to gather delicious local artisan cheeses. The team would also like to thank Foreign Cinema restaurant and Universal Café in San Francisco, California.

Weldon Owen also wishes to thank the following individuals for their kind assistance: Desne Ahlers, Ken DellaPenta, Harriet Docker, Judith Dunham, Jean-Blaise Hall, Nigel James, Ashley Johnson, Denise Santoro Lincoln, Louise Mackaness, Norma MacMillan, Andrea Meyer, Paul Moore, Lesli Neilson, Joan Olson, and Leon Yu.

PHOTO CREDITS

Quentin Bacon, all photography, except for the following:
Paul Moore: Front cover (bottom)
©PictureNet/CORBIS: Front cover (top)
Bruce Stoddard/Getty Images: Endpapers

PHOTOGRAPHY LOCATIONS

The following New York locations have been given references for the map on pages 30–31.

Bonnier Books

BONNIER BOOKS

Appledram Barns
Birdham Road
Chichester, West Sussex
PO20 7EQ

FOODS OF THE WORLD NEW YORK

Originally published as
Williams-Sonoma Foods of the World New York

Conceived and produced by Weldon Owen Inc.
814 Montgomery Street, San Francisco, CA 94133
Telephone: 415-291-0100 Fax: 415-291-8841

In Collaboration with Williams-Sonoma, Inc.
3250 Van Ness Avenue, San Francisco, CA 94109

A Weldon Owen Production
Copyright © 2006 Weldon Owen Inc.
and Williams-Sonoma, Inc.

First printed in 2006
10 9 8 7 6 5 4 3 2 1

ISBN 978-1905825-09-7

Printed by Tien Wah Press
Printed in Singapore

WELDON OWEN INC.

Chief Executive Officer John Owen
President and Chief Operating Officer Terry Newell
Vice President International Sales Stuart Laurence
Vice President and Creative Director Gaye Allen
Vice President and Publisher Hannah Rahill
Series Editor Kim Goodfriend
Editorial Assistant Juli Vendzules

Art Director Nicky Collings
Designers Alison Fenton, Rachel Lopez

Production Director Chris Hemesath
Colour Specialist Teri Bell
Production and Reprint Coordinator Todd Rechner

Food Stylist George Dolese
Associate Food Stylist Elisabet der Nederlanden
Prop Stylists Marina Malchin, Laura Ferguson
Photographer's Assistants Amy Sims, Brooke Buchanan
Map Illustrator Bart Wright
Translator Josephine Bacon